REBELS

OF

KINDNESS

Aaron Ableman

REBELS

OF

KINDNESS

How Loving-Care Transforms Self,
Others and Planet

BY AARON ABLEMAN & JUSTIN WILKENFELD

SCAN THE QR CODE BELOW
FOR MORE "REBELS OF KINDNESS"
STORIES, SWAG AND ADVENTURES IN BENEVOLENCE

ADVANCE PRAISE

"Rebels of Kindness strikes a mindful balance of science and creativity. Ableman & Wilkenfeld spotlight leaders from every walk of life who are changing the world through compassion while providing thought-provoking narratives and practical exercises to turn inspiration into application. This counter-cultural mindset of kindness is necessary to help to create a better world."

—Houston Kraft, Author of *Deep Kindness*

"Rebels of Kindness is a book I wish America and the world had many decades back. At this difficult time in our history where violence and hatred and division and mean-spiritedness have become as natural as breathing for many, it is so clear to me that what we need are different kinds of blueprints for our humanity, for our collective soul. This book, through its real-life stories, takes us on a fantastical journey of what is possible for you, me, for all of us, if we simply overstand, as we say, that kindness—and love—is a practice worth practicing every single day of our lives."

—Kevin Powell, civil and human rights activist, poet, filmmaker, author of 16 books

"Rebels Of Kindness combines cutting-edge science, human values and joyful creativity, all with the simplicity that anyone can vibe with! This book explores all of that through the epic stories of those behind an increasingly mainstream movement toward altruism. As any post-apocalyptic meme maker or storyteller knows, we need a mainstream "reSTORYation" across all sectors. Doesn't love, compassion and kindness seem like good places to start? Please join me in supporting the important work of Mr Ableman and Mr Wilkenfeld as they write the next pages in a more beautiful and fulfilling book of life!"

—Ryland Engelheart, Filmmaker & CoFounder @ Kiss The Ground

"Aaron Ableman's heart is ablaze with activism. Weaving in music, art and his infectious love for Mother Earth, Aaron joins forces with Justin Wilkenfeld to make wisdom accessible and entertaining to all ages. Rebels of Kindness is a how-to-change-the-world book, asking us each to simply stretch beyond our comforts and fears and water our own communities with more compassion. Be careful; wherever you see this book, there's a revolution afoot!"

—Jon Marro: Artist, Author & Creativity Coach

"Our dear brothers of the planet gently walk us into the lap of love. For true love is love-in-action. And this type of kindness is most accessible through a loving heart and still mind. Each story in this book gives both adults and children a chance to be moved by human goodness and then literally practice it through meditation, reflection or action. It's a creative and inspired approach to teaching the most powerful human virtue: compassion. One story a day from Rebels of Kindness is just what your heart may want and definitely what the world needs."

—Nimo Patel, Kindness Advocate & Indian Hip-Hop Star

"In a world of suffering, where low vibration energy is plentiful, it takes courage to stay kind. This beautiful book shows such a spirit: rebels of kindness blazing trails with their powerful acts of positivity. Their service is a beacon of light, allowing the glimmering goodness to radiate and multiply. When we acknowledge these individuals and their courage to make the world a better place, we allow for a deeper understanding of how kindness can truly transform our planet. Together we make a difference."

—Leigh Clark, Author & Founder @ Kindleigh

REBELS OF KINDNESS

How Loving-Care Transforms Self, Others and Planet

AARON ABLEMAN & JUSTIN WILKENFELD

FREEDOM

THREE
PUBLISHING

kindhumans

COPYRIGHT 2023

ISBN: 979-8-9877429-1-4

Library of Congress Control Number: 2023902271

TABLE OF CONTENTS

ACKNOWLEDGMENTS

Aaron would like to thank life itself, the evolutionary love impulse of existence. Aaron also sends massive gratitude to immediate family - e.g. beloveds Chaya, Erika, Donna, Jeanne-Marie and Michael - who have put kindness, unconditional love and good humor to the test since day 1. Thanks to all the people who have supported the work of altruistic and heart-centered culture-building throughout the years of endless projects in Aaron's career. Hugs of appreciation to the generous and brilliant community who helped birth this work directly, especially the spirited Joel Harper, Kevin Tharpe and Jen Philips Johnson who helped mobilize to make this book a reality. Thanks to Dylan Hirsch-Shell, for supporting this project with such profound generosity and strategic upliftment - there's no way it would have happened otherwise. Ultimately, thanks to the billions of unsung heroes, who choose care instead of violence and love instead of fear without getting noticed or thanked; you're the reason to wake up with a smile and unwavering faith.

Justin would like to thank everyone, grammatically speaking, in the 1st person! So ... thanks to my family, Suzi, Quinn, Noa - especially for all the love and magnetic joy they bring to those who know them. Thanks to my parents, Holly and Jason for adopting and loving him. Thanks to Kyla, Aurora, all the cousins, aunts, uncles, and extended family! Thanks to my biological parents for bringing me into this world. Thanks to all my friends who have helped carry the load and for making life fun! Thanks to the Kindhumans team and community for your love and support as we have been trying to build a platform for kindness. Thanks to the ocean for grounding me in nature and the glory that is life itself. Thanks to the community of environmental stewards around the globe protecting the 7 seas to the highest peaks! Thanks to all my ancestors and my predecessors...we continue to build on the human experience in hopes of finding our inner peace and harmony with our world and all this beautiful life in it. Thanks to humans around the globe prioritizing kindness in their daily lives, no matter how hard or challenging it may get. I am grateful to have the opportunity to wake up each day to experience life and I hope that everyone can find their unique spark for life. I want to acknowledge that I appreciate each and every person that has shaped my existence. It has been profound and while I cannot possibly ever thank you all personally, know that you have affected me personally, and on a deep level. Your humanity shines through. I truly love you all, my fellow humans and my real hope is that we can find kindness in our hearts and common ground in our shared humanity.

DEDICATION

This book goes out to all kind humans

rising above the pessimism of society.

those who are dedicated to finding common ground

with folks who are different,

turning losses to lessons

and transforming hate into motivation

for loving even louder.

A WISH

"My wish for you is that you continue.

Continue to be who and how you are,

to astonish a mean world with your acts of kindness."

~Maya Angelou~

FOREWORD

It seems that in our current political and social milieu, fear, anger, blame, shame, and 'othering' are the order of the day. This energy so proliferates throughout the media and on social media that sometimes, the most courageous thing a person can be in this type of environment is kind, loving, and compassionate. These qualities are the true gifts and nature of the Spirit that indwells us. They allow us to see through the vitriol and acknowledge the innate goodness within each person and underneath every circumstance, regardless of appearance and form.

Enter Rebels of Kindness, a treatise of inspiring personal stories, poetry, prayers, and practices illustrating that not only do we absolutely live in a benevolent and loving-Universe, our role here on Earth is to co-create and amplify that Reality. It demonstrates that yes, kindness is a virtue, but it is also a choice. And the more of us who choose to be kind and loving in each of the small moments that make up our daily lives and experiences, the more we expand our role in being a beneficial presence on the planet.

As you dive into these heartening stories and engage in these uplifting practices, your heart and mind will expand, and the dynamic peace and harmony that is Life itself will rise up in and radiate through you. And as this happens, you, as well as the world will be blessed.

Michael Bernard Beckwith

Founder & CEO, Agape International Spiritual Center
Author, Life Visioning and Spiritual Liberation

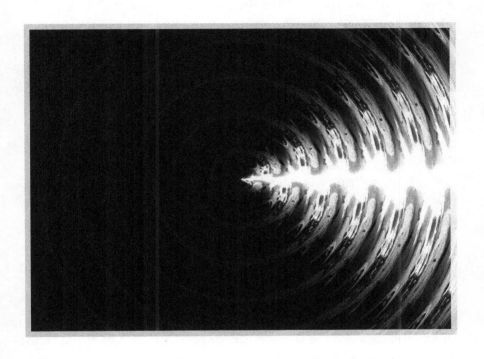

THE OLD WOMAN & THE TREE

Ever heard the parable of the old woman who planted a tree that educated an entire town? The story goes like this: when this old woman was not yet old, but just a young girl of 9 years, there was a horrendous storm. An old oak tree next to her bedroom was knocked down in the maelstrom of lightning, thunder, and gale winds. This tree had been important to her; she loved to climb it, to listen to it rustling, and to enjoy its shade. She was heartbroken that her beloved tree was now destroyed. The next day, she ran out to the shattered trunk, rummaging for acorns amidst the splintered wood and windblown leaves. She found a few with tan skin that appeared undamaged and she stuck them in her pocket like a squirrel before wintertime · or a rebel who refuses to let what she loves die.

Later that week, while walking by an abandoned field, she remembered the seeds in her pocket! On a whim, she decided to plant these acorns in the field. Saying a quiet thank you to the earth, she watered the seeds with her little water bottle and then sang a sweet song. For almost two months, on her way home from school, she watered them in the same way. One full moon, a little sprout popped up and began growing. But not too long after this spontaneous act of kindness, she moved far away because of her dad's new job. As time passed, she forgot all about the old oak tree, its destruction, and the tiny sprouts that had emerged.

Fast forward many long years later... she came back to her hometown to visit for the first time since she left. After being flooded with memories long forgotten, she went to find the abandoned field to see if her tree had grown. Shockingly, she saw an enormous, grand oak tree larger than a building! There were kids and families playing underneath it, butterflies with bees dancing in the branches, and beautiful community gardens flourishing underneath. Not only that, but a city park had been established, honoring the tree for having become a source of joy, education, and beauty for the entire town.

Under the tree, a sign read:

"Trees remind us of the good things in life: to breathe deeply, to love each other and create beauty with what we have, where we are, and with what time is given to us. Let's all learn from these ancient teachers, from ElemenTree school to UniversiTree!"

The old woman started laughing and crying at the same time. No one ever knew she planted that tree, but that didn't matter. The pure act of giving and receiving life was enough for her.

Pop culture often misses the stories of these life-nourishing fables (and the real-life versions of them), despite kind heroes in every community from here to Timbuktu. Not those who are airbrushed or perfect. Not superheroes. Not those who are rich or technically knowledgeable, but those that distinguish themselves by the size of their hearts. We are talking about those who live with daily intentions to do good, to treat people well, and to make the world a better place - even when they falter, fall, or make mistakes. This work is dedicated to those who go out to change that world with their imperfect but profound gifts of loving kindness!

INTENTIONS

It costs nothing to be kind, so maybe that's why economists and politicians have made it worthless for much of modern human history. Funny but not funny, right? We've been living in a money-driven world for so long that the sheer concept of living for other reasons, like spreading love and kindness, seems almost laughable to say out loud. This appears especially true amongst big government and big business, who are ironically those driving our systems, infrastructures and institutions. Even if it were to make them more money by being kind, the jury is out on whether it would become the standard. But this begs a more serious question: are humans faltering in systemic ways simply because of an inverted approach to life itself?

This complex history of humanity raises many questions about our collective past, present, and future. Like can we learn from civilizations that crashed and burned or is topsy-turvey entropy just an unavoidable force at larger scales? Or can we change for the better and evolve a more life-honoring governance rooted in respect and mutual-benefit? Will systemic non-violence and moral courage ever emerge as mainstream priorities for our collective survival? Is the climate and biodiversity crisis the push needed to reimagine, redesign, and re-invest in systems of creativity, empathy and love?

Whether on a big or small scale, we humans often try to dominate our way to success, believing that what's outside of us is the problem and the best way to solve it is through fighting or forcing. However, the only thing we can ultimately control is ourselves (though also questionable), and this is best done through loving-care. So maybe our attempt to dominate or win it all would be more successful if it was based on empowered people coming together in "coopetition" and service for the greater good?

From teaching classrooms to running governments, cross-disciplinary evidence shows us that kindness is directly linked to the preservation of life. This applies to our own lives, the lives of our children, and the lives of generations to come. Ask any caring parent or caregiver! Just because it takes some extra intention and work, doesn't mean we should give up hope that the future continues to improve in a positive way and that we can be part of a continuum of healing rather than continuing to hurt others and the planet in a blind quest for aggrandizement. With a bit of vision adjustment, we can vastly improve our lives, our communities, or our relationship with the greater cosmos. It just takes practice!

That's why inside the pages of this book are more than philosophies. These are real-life stories of humans who embody a thesis of kindness as praxis. These are the heroes of an emergent paradigm, beloved for their ability to enlighten themselves, care for others and regenerate our ecosystems. We have identified an initial group of exemplars, who span geography, age, race, culture, and political views. If we're lucky, this book will proliferate many other stories and books about kind heroes in communities everywhere, until we register them in a Library Of Kindness.

Rebels of kindness are as old as time and as numerous as grains of sand on a beach. They are everywhere goodness lives. They are the center and circumference of the world. They are unflinching and resilient. They are optimistic in the face of unspeakable challenges. And though they are just as imperfect as any other human who has ever walked this earth, rebels of kindness are champions of the human spirit. We only wish we could give a voice to them all, but living and sharing their message is a task for all of us, as we take this storytelling into our own lives.

The great humanitarian and mathematician Albert Einstein once said: "I think the most important question facing humanity is, is the universe a friendly place?" Despite those who would argue this, we, the rebels, believe the answer is "YES!" but only if we are willing to create it through authentic exploration, understanding, and altruism. Through the wisdom of the courageous humans inside this book, we hope to inspire you on a magical path of kindness, creativity, and connection.

~~~~~~

KINDNESS TO SELF

~~~~~~

CIRCLE OF KINDNESS

KINDNESS

FAITH PRESENCE HUMILITY

CREATIVITY LISTENING COMPASSION FORGIVENESS SERVICE

WONDER VULNERABILITY REST BREATH GRATITUDE JOY SELF-CARE PATIENCE HUMOR PERSEVERANCE

INNER=SELF MIDDLE=OTHERS OUTER=PLANET

KINDNESS TO SELF

Engaging in acts of self-kindness is a "nutrient stacked life-enhancement drug" (without the silly name or price tag!) since it yields endorphins to cultivate mental health and physical wellness. Additionally, it can impact the reduction of stress because perpetually kind people have 23% less cortisol - that's the stress hormone.

A University of British Columbia study screened a large group of highly anxious individuals who performed at least six acts of self-kindness a week. After only four weeks, there was a significant increase in confidence, positivity, relationship satisfaction, and a drastic drop in social avoidance for these timid or anxious individuals.

Amazingly, Stephen Post (of Case Western Reserve University School of Medicine) found that when we practice caring for ourselves and our relationships, everything from life satisfaction to self-realization and physical health is wildly improved. Lifespan's are lengthened, melancholy or woefulness is reduced, and well-being is greatly increased.

Acts of self-care and kindness to self lowers blood pressure and helps the body create a "cardioprotective" hormone. Loving yourself is a foundational form of holistic medicine!

Like the sun rising over the highest mountain

I see that the light is I, a gold dawn fountain;

As I open my heart to the truth, I take a breather

I am my best student, my best teacher!

I give love to all because I am also the receiver!

I'm alive because of you, infinity and countin'

I am love myself, becoming a kind human now and again.

9

S.N. GOENKA

"Rather than converting people from one organized religion to another organized religion, we should try to convert people from misery to happiness, from bondage to liberation and from cruelty to compassion."

A disciple once demanded of the Buddha what to do about the infinity of the world. The Buddha responded simply: "Whether the world is finite or infinite, limited or unlimited, the problem of your liberation remains the same." In other words, our time is too short to fantasize about unanswerable questions, especially if our day to day lives are lost in ego and greed.

A similar approach to life was pioneered by the great teacher and bringer of mindfulness to the west, Mr S.N. Goenka. As a boy born to an affluent family of Indian ancestry, Goenka was raised in Myanmar and became a successful businessman with great power in the private sector. Yet for some reason, he felt stuck, angry and often thought only about himself. It was at that point that he started experiencing crushing migraine headaches and no medical doctors could find a cure. At the behest of a friend, he met with a Vipassana teacher named Sayagyi U Ba Khin and persisted with this teacher for 14 years of deep study. Conscious breathing and awareness of the thoughts that control our lives were two of the core elements of his learning journey.

Becoming a tireless rebel of kindness and compassion, Mr Goenka moved to India and began teaching Vipassana to whomsoever wished to learn. But he was residing in a country cruel in its divisions between caste or religion, so a meditative school designed 'for anyone who can breathe' was an indignity to the society. Mr. Goenka paid it no mind (pun intended) and soon attracted thousands of people from every part of the nation. His radically inclusive teachings drew people from countries all over the world to come and experience the power of meditation.

Over a half century later, with decades of daily teachings on the power of breath and mind, Mr. Goenka and the teachers he taught hundreds of thousands of people in India and around the planet. At the time of this writing, meditation centers established under his guidance are still operating in Asia, Europe, the Americas and Africa, years after his death.

The practice taught by Mr Goenka goes back two and a half millennia to the Buddha himself. The Buddha never taught religion; he taught truth – a pathway to inner freedom which is ubiquitous to the human experience. In the same tradition, Mr. Goenka's approach is totally open and available to all. For this reason, his teaching has had a profound appeal to people of all backgrounds, of every religion and no religion, and from every part of the world.

If you can't make a 10 day silent retreat (though highly recommended and encouraged for everyone on earth!), try this 10 minute Vipassana-inspired meditation right now:

1. Find a quiet and comfortable place to sit, with your back straight and your eyes closed.
2. Begin by focusing on your breath, noticing the sensation of the breath as it enters and exits your nose. As you focus on your breath, try to let go of any thoughts or

distractions that arise. If your mind wanders, gently bring your attention back to your breath. Over and over and over again.

3. Continue to focus on your breath for the entire 10 minutes, or for as long as you are able.

4. When the time is over, take a deep breath and slowly open your eyes.

It's important to remember that meditation is a practice (not "a perfect") and it can take time to develop the ability to focus and train the wild monkey that is the human mind. It's okay if your mind wanders during the practice; that's normal. Be kind and gentle with yourself—you are learning a new skill!

SELF-LOVE TRIBUTE

To love myself is the beginning

Of a life-long dance, rhythm-a-ning.

But to love another is the ending

Of this life long loneliness thing.

How do I find a way when

their opposites are tugging?

My loving me is what justice

feels like ... Ouroboros!

But loving you is what mustard does with mayonnaise

So delicious it's unafraid to share the tastiness.

The crack of your lip's flavor exposes writ

Large, until life becomes soul food - a poet's music.

You teach me that two is one, an infinite script.

Maybe trinity is within us all: we are the love we seek, isn't it?

Everyone's said it all before, the universe gets quoted,

Nature is the author of us all in motion:

Summertime, wintertime.

The beginning is my finish line.

The path is my destination.

My attitude defines success, let love win.

Aren't we all just needing love's medicine?

And love is the key to heaven's door, let it in.

LORETTA AFRAID OF BEAR COOK

"I consider myself a culture bearer, a keeper of the old ways, and I say that because I became a grandmother. I have a beautiful grandson, and I think it's important to know these things..."

Grandmother Loretta is a Lakota medicine woman and Sundance leader who is a walking encyclopedia of knowledge, wisdom, and kindness. Loretta grew up on the Pine Ridge Reservation where she was immersed in Lakota culture and language. Thanks to family and the elders who trained her, she is considered a holder of key ancestral knowledge, including the Tiospaye's Sundance pipe. Her fierce and courageous spirit is evident in her long-standing activism for the betterment of herself, her people and the planet.

Loretta's activism began in her 20s, when she participated in the Trail of Broken Treaties, a protest in which 800 Natives occupied the Bureau of Indian Affairs headquarters in Washington, D.C. during a crucial federal election week in November 1972. The 20-point proposal paper that was presented during this protest became the basis for Native American tribal lands restoration, cross-cultural reconciliation, and future reconstruction strategies across "Indian Country" ever since. Sixteen of the 20 points have been resolved in the 47 years since that time!

Loretta has made history again and again through her efforts. Some of her "herstoric" efforts have included gathering a consensus to call for the return of the Black Hills sacred lands to the people of the Great Sioux Nation, which was presented to the White House. She also assisted in passing the 1975 Indian Self-Determination and Educational Assistance Act, the American Indian Freedom of Religion Act of 1978, and its subsequent amendments!

More recently, Loretta was one of 12 Native delegates collaborating with "The Long March to Rome," a continuation of a 40-year movement to get the Vatican to address the "papal bull of May 4, 1493" as representative of a series of 15th-century decrees that became the Doctrine of Christian Domination. This horrific doctrine called for the invasion, capture, and enslavement of pagan nations in order to benefit Western Christendom. In 1992, the Indigenous Law Institute began a campaign to revoke these decrees and Loretta was among the prominent Native American activists who signed a joint statement to the Pontifical Council for Justice and Peace. This statement ultimately led to the "Long March to Rome" gathering in 2016, where Loretta and 11 other Native delegates met with Pope Francis in St. Peter's Square. During this historic meeting, Loretta spoke directly to the Pope and requested that he revoke, rescind, and do away with the May 4, 1493 Inter Caetera Papal Bulls. To her surprise, the Pope replied with a simple but powerful "Yes."

Loretta, along with her husband Tom Kanatakeniate Cook, oversaw the Slim Buttes Agricultural Development program on the Pine Ridge reservation for years. She and her husband, Tom, share a life-long commitment to improving daily life for her people and her Tiospaye. Above all the spiritual and social achievements, she is most proud of her service to young people in discovering and living their beautiful culture, but also reviving the sacred Oglala ceremonies that keep life alive for all.

15

Her own life is a tremendous example that service to others is serving oneself and serving oneself also serves others. It's all connected and all important.

Here's a non-denominational prayer to share, inspired by Grandmother Loretta and her tradition:

> "Great Spirit, I embrace my healing power to touch the earth, the water, the air, and all living things. I hold the bright faith that I help my people to respect and take care of the earth and all its inhabitants, so that we may live in harmony and balance. I am not separate from your healing and you're not separate from mine.
>
> We remember ourselves and the earth as sacred and worthy of timeless respect. We hold a covenant that we care for the earth as we would care for our own bodies. We walk lightly upon the earth and leave no more traces than the rain, faith and kindness.
>
> Spirit, we thank you for your guidance and wisdom as we work to heal the earth and all its inhabitants. By opening our hearts and minds to healing and restoration, we ask that you bless us with the determination to make a positive difference in the world, and to leave a legacy of kindness and respect for future generations.
>
> Aho Mitakuye Oyasin. We are all related. And so it is."

This prayer is one example that was adapted from a call with Grandmother Loretta, but there are many other ways to pray or express love for your life or that of life itself. Different cultures and spiritual traditions have their own ways to express this spiritual connection, it is important to choose the one that resonates with you or is authentically given to you to use.

SELF-CARE AFFIRMATIONS

I embrace the blessing of what is.

Gratitude is my every moment attitude.

I am grateful for whatever I have and don't have.

I seek to find the positive in any situation.

I aim to uncover the best qualities in myself and others.

I am learning to be bigger than my worries or my fears.

I cherish and embrace the precious time I have on this planet.

I eat nutritious foods, drink clean water
and stop to smell the flowers.

I am more than my body, my name or my story.

I embrace presence, a gift, my being present is enough to
succeed at anything.

I face my frontiers of pain with the vulnerability of a medicine
person.

As I truly release the past, I discover I have nothing to run or
hide from.

I am the peace and love I seek; true peace and true love seeks
to envelop me.

I am my ancestors' service and my descendants embrace.

In times of anxiety or stress, I choose to breathe and smile;
calming my nervous system is changing the world.

I act as if I make a difference because my life matters.

I am the wonder of the universe and the universe is wonderful.

I am a child of god, god is the activity of my consciousness.

DEVI BROWN

"You don't want to try to control every aspect of your life, then there is no room for God"

Devi Brown was raised by a low-income single mother in Los Angeles and learned to depend on herself as an only child. Moving house from place to place or dealing with instability at home may have been what pushed her to uncover a deeper purpose in life. Such childhood experience actually made her more flexible to change and exposed her to new ideas that she might never have otherwise been exposed to, like when a family friend introduced her to Buddhism and chanting at a very young age. Imagine a young child facing such instability but choosing to meditate and chant instead. This tug of war between the pushes of the world and the pulls of her inner voice became a common theme throughout her healing journey.

Over time, she grew into a charismatic and kind-hearted businesswoman, rising through the ranks of the radio-media industry, from intern to host! But as the demands of success tossed her left and right, she forgot her early anchor in spirituality or self-care. Sadly, she developed a stress-induced burnout that sent her searching for deeper solutions to mental health. The paradox of being highly successful on the outside and yet hurting in pain on the inside is something she has spoken vulnerably about to illuminate the slippery path of worldly success without inner fortitude. Whether it's Twitch or Robin Williams, Mac Miller or Kate Spade, one doesn't have to look far for examples of how dangerous it can be to dishonor the voices of pain or confusion inside our hearts and minds.

At the peak of Devi's struggle, tumbling through a rocky marriage and cross-country relocation, she prayed to God. Shortly thereafter, a friend suggested she try out a meditation retreat. She went on a 10 day silent retreat with no phone - an impossibility for her 24/7 connected and fast paced life! As the saying goes: the only way out is to go in! And that's what she did. Using timeless techniques of breathwork, prayer and movement, she talks about how that retreat was a major turning point in her adult life, the shift that helped integrate a successful media brand with her lifelong passion for self-love and self-liberation.

Since Brown's awakening and reset, she has gone deep into studying wellness and wisdom traditions from around the globe. Noting that she's often been the only woman of color in these learning spaces, she has emphasized inviting more diverse communities, especially since they're often the ones who get left out of their own traditional healing ways. From custom-made crystal instruments used to clear energetic blocks to journaling practices to ceremonial rituals focused on healing generational trauma, Devi facilitates similar wellness practices that got her through tough times. As a seasoned broadcaster and host of her own podcast, Devi uses transformative conversation and storytelling to help amplify spiritual psychology, meditation and much more.

A crystalline invitation to take into your life: try going to a local metaphysical store, crystal shop or just a favorite location with crystal rocks in nature. Once you arrive, whether it's asking for help calming your anxiety or recovering from a traumatic event, set an intention to heal whatever you're struggling with. Have faith that it's already done and done well! Next, if you're able, start to soften your eyes and gently rub your hands over the stones that are all around you to choose a crystal to aid in your healing journey.

Please note that your own mind may start to judge or comment on the silly-pseudoscience ridiculousness of this activity using modern witchcraft for medicinal or wellness purposes. You can encourage your mental chatter or opinions to relax for a moment with a few deep breaths. Ask yourself honestly: doesn't my mind have the ability to heal? Researchers at the National Library Of Medicine have studied the placebo effect on illness and interpersonal healing. They've stated that the placebo effect is distinct from natural spontaneous healing, homeopathic medicine or from the aid of medication or procedures. It can heal conditions or disorders, even when the person knows they're taking a placebo! So, now you can trust your activity by way of this research.

Back to the stones. Find one that feels great to your hand and then consult the shopkeeper (or any books on crystals) to get more information on the properties that these crystals carry. Celestite might help calm anxiety, especially before bedtime. Rose quartz has a long tradition of being used for self-love and cultivating faith in oneself. Once you've got your crystal, you can clean it with water and then start to meditate or pray with it whenever you see fit.

BEING, HUMAN, BEING

We all struggle with being human.
We cry over onions and losing games.
We get mad over traffic and bad politics.
We get frustrated because we base our level of success
strictly on external results.
We assign our happiness to some time in the future
when our mortgage is finally paid off,
when our relationships are finally healed
and when our dreams finally come true.
We fall apart because the worries or doubts of life
shake us off center.
And it's no wonder.
It's not easy to swim through
a stormy ocean of bills, emergencies or responsibilities.
Nonetheless, we persist.
And the old metaphorical story of the lotus flower might be
helpful to share why we do ...
The lotus flower is one of the most fragrant and voluptuous
flowers on the face of the earth.
Yet, ironically, it grows from the dirtiest and muckiest mud.
The lotus pushes its way through the mud, rising toward the
sun's light above the element from whence it was born.
As the lotus bud first emerges at the water's surface,
the first petal opens.
A lotus is a rebel of kindness, revolting against the forces of
gravity or despair, rising from the darkness to become an
uncanny perfume and food source for all of nature.
We all have the same qualities of the lotus.
Or a rebel of kindness.
We can all relate to the journey of darkness to light,
of womb to new life, of struggle to liberation, of violence to care.

ELOUISE OLIVER

"In the baseball game of life, you are the referee and you call the shots."

Born dirt poor in the swamps of Florida with grandparents who were slaves, Elouise Oliver taught herself how to read with an old bible and developed prophetic visions of bringing people together from all walks of life. Spoiler alert: her visions would come true almost 70 years later! She learned to love nature as a child, witnessing how medicinal plants would grow wild with no cultivation in the places they were needed most for the ailments of the humans that lived there. Dandelion, a liver cleanser, grew wild all around the bars where alcoholics ran. Oat's Straw and St John's Wort, best for helping cure addiction and depression, would grow around the tobacco shops.

After growing up and becoming a nurse, she married a man in the military and lived all over the world, rearing 7 children! One day, one of her kids encouraged her to come check out a spiritual community called "Science Of Mind". The Science Of Mind movement - grounded by its church communities around the world called "Centers For Spiritual Living" - was founded by Ernest Holmes, a mystic in the early transcendentalist movement with Ralph Waldo Emerson. The philosophy is best summed up by Ernest: "Each person is an individualized center of God-conscious life and divine action. Each is a unique individualization. When people obey the dictates of the inner voice, they find every pathway open before them." This depth of wisdom was a lightbulb of inspiration and alchemy for Elouise. She and her son, the Reverend Muata, studied for years in practitioner and ministerial schools along with master teachers. After decades of study and practice, they became ministers and champions for this perennial philosophy.

As a spiritual leader, the essence of her ministry is about the power and practice of unconditional love. She teaches that love and forgiveness are the answers to all human discord. Bringing people in off the streets, offering birth, wedding and death ceremonies and facilitating affirmative prayer classes, Reverend Elouise has helped heal thousands of people around the globe. There's a story of a young man about to commit suicide who came to her class with a weapon in his pocket only to be coerced into trying meditation ... and his life changed almost instantaneously and miraculously, eventually becoming a leading expert for others struggling with mental health issues. "Ask me how I know...the truth of self-love and meditation will set you free..." the Reverend told him at the choicepoint of his weighing life vs death.

Known lovingly by the moniker "Rev E", she has received widespread street recognition for the fierce kindness she gives so generously! She has inspired the building of more than 30 churches and empowered followers to become leaders around the globe. Now at the youthful age of 95, she eats an organic alkaline diet, meditates everyday, writes books and holds prayer vigils with community leaders. She emphasizes the importance of self-love and financial literacy, which are often overlooked in traditional education. In her own words, "The only things we don't teach in schools are self-love, nutrition and financial literacy. It's time to get back to the basics."

A practical takeaway, inspired by "Rev E":

1. Find a comfortable seated position and close your eyes. Take 10 deep breaths and allow yourself to settle into the present moment.
2. Bring to mind a person or experience that brings you feelings of love and admiration. It could be a loved one, a pet, or a memory of a special moment. Allow yourself to fully immerse in these feelings of kindness.
3. As you continue to focus on this experience or person, begin to extend these feelings of love and acceptance to yourself. Allow yourself to fully embrace self-love and self-acceptance.
4. Repeat to yourself, either out loud or silently: "I am worthy of love and acceptance. I am enough just as I am. I deeply and completely love and accept myself." Feel the truth of these statements in your heart, whether your mind accepts them yet or not. Take a few more deep breaths and allow yourself to sink deeper into this self-love and self-acceptance. Allow yourself to fully soak in these feelings.
5. When you are ready, slowly open your eyes and take a moment to journal about your experience. What did you notice during the meditation? How do you feel now?

Remember that self-love is a journey and you don't have to have it figured out yet. Be patient as you continue unpeeling the onion layers of yourself, ever focused on nurturing the ancient core of love within.

AN OLD STORY

There're is an old story about a sage who stood in front of an audience with an orange and asked:

"What will come out of this if I squeeze it?"

A child said: "Orange juice, of course!"

The sage responded: "Exactly! But humans also have a kind of juice inside us which I like to call *'conscious-juice'.* Whatever we go through in our lives-whether it's tragedy or a triumph-our experience squeezes the juice inside us all. But unlike the orange, what's inside the human is what we choose to create.

Will you choose to be bitter or sweet?"

JACOB COLLIER

"I grew up in this room filled with musical instruments, but most importantly, I had a family who encouraged me to invest in my own imagination, and so things I created, things I built were good things to be building just because I was making them..."

Being part of a family of successful musicians is nice and all. But have you ever tried coming from a family of successful musicians who also invite everyone around them into their discipline, process and purpose behind the music? That's like winning the lottery while discovering the key to lasting wealth is to give it away! That's like being the chosen one but choosing to anoint the community around you as well! This isn't just a moral thought experiment either, it's a real life framework for understanding Mr. Jacob Collier. Jacob's combination of supportive family and hardworking talent is amplified by the kindness and humility he stands for.

Jacob was immersed in music since Age 0, where hums, tones and scales might have been a 2nd breast milk. He learned to play various instruments with the tireless support of his loving mother, Suzi. In his family's wildly creative home, Jacob grew into a unique and original artist with the humility of a monk and the aptitude of a modern Mozart. "I was brought up by women," he says with a smile. "I was encouraged to see the world in this way where everything is a question." Using a split-screen recording technique, Jacob records himself singing and playing

27

a myriad of instruments in a variety of styles, from jazz to classical, ancient to modern. He's pioneered a particular passion for polyrhythms, close harmony, dissonance, and microtonality, and over his career, has helped to revitalize interest in complex music appreciation for mainstream audiences.

After being discovered by the iconic Quincy Jones, Jacob has toured the world and won Grammy Awards but still wears a blue wig or pajamas into label meetings with executives and lawyers. He often teaches classes on his own unusual creative processes, on revolutionizing music theory for wider communities and on the importance of retaining a human element in this age of tech-dominant music making. Since his platform has grown to great influence, he often posts activist videos or humanitarian statements on issues ranging from voting rights to climate justice. In the last two U.S democratic elections, he posted a video of him playing notes on the piano that then visually generated the message VOTE!, in musical notation format, on the computer program he is using to record.

Above all the accolades, however, his greatest gift is his kind heart and his love for bringing friends and community along the learning journey of life. Imagine being a superstar on television but still taking the train into the depths of South Brooklyn for a friend's gig whenever he's in town! Jacob prioritizes ministration above acquisition, taking the time to support young or struggling artists and performing with his mother for the pure joy of it. Without it being forced or calculated, Jacob Collier is creating a new archetype for celebrities that's founded on kindness and generosity.

A sonic takeaway, inspired by Jacob: experiment in how to create dynamic, pleasurable and bellowing tones with your voice. Start with creating a safe space for yourself. Get present by sitting or standing comfortably and then close your eyes with a giant smile on your face. Now ask an intentional or imaginative question for your practice like "If the universe is vibrational, who am I?"

Now take a deep breath, and on the exhale, allow a sound to come out of your mouth. You can try starting with a simple vowel sound, such as "ah," and holding the sound for as long as you comfortably can. As you make the sound, try to focus on the vibration of the sound and how it feels in your body. You can bring in subtle melodic or rhythmic experiments but try to stick with sustained vowel sounds or extended tones (even guttural or awkward tones to challenge notions of "music" are great).

Another way to use sonic or musically-inspired techniques for self-healing is to engage in instrument-toning. This can be done with any instrument that can easily sustain a single note, such as a guitar, singing bowl, a didgeridoo, or a gong. To do this, hold the instrument in a relaxed position and take a deep breath; on the exhale, allow the sound to come out of the instrument. As you make the sound, focus on the vibration of the sound as it reverberates and interacts with your mind-body-spirit.

Toning and sound exploration can be a powerful tool for self-healing because it provides a sense of relaxation, stress reduction and inner peace.

CHOOSE YOU

What if life is a movie called muse,
channeled & written by you, not a spoof!

All plot lines are self-generated too,
even the failures or villains you do.

Do you choose change or does change choose you?

Every motive hints at the next clue,
like a who-done-it about water - don't pollute -
and do unto others downstream as you
would have others upstream do unto you.

Every character relationship matters too,
every heart, every current is a million shades of blue.

Do you care for what cares for you?

Against or with the tide, will you
swim your inner hero's journey, boo boo?

SADGHURU

"The most beautiful moments in life are moments when you are
expressing your joy, not when you are seeking it."

Stereotypes or cliched tropes of the guru archetype might benefit
the media by reproducing a fantastical story, but they often don't
reflect the complexity and nuance of such a teacher's life nor true
purpose. They also don't allow audiences or students to connect
with the deeper traumas, triumphs and teachings that may have
shaped that guru's healing message in the first place. This
background is important to consider when delving into any
important teacher in your life - whether they're a secular mentor
or a celebrity guru. And finally, there's nothing like sitting with
a master teacher (if they're alive) for a real dharma talk, a deep
meditation or a prolonged period of study.

Sadghuru, like many gurus in India, incarnated into a normal
family in a small village. His birth name was Jaggi, and he was
born to a humble but well-off family of scholars and homemakers
in the town of Mysore, India. Jaggi's father was a doctor and his
mother was a homemaker. His mother's lineage traced back to
the legendary Indian ruler and polyglot, Krishnadeva Raya, and
it was at his mother's ancestral home that Jaggi met with the
master yogi and teacher, Malladihalli Sri Raghavendra, who
introduced him to the ancient art of yoga. This experience led to
a daily practice of asana and pranayama throughout his youth.

From a young age, Jaggi was quite different from other children in his family, exploring the natural world like a yogic daredevil. He enjoyed roaming in the jungle, smelling under rocks to catch venomous snakes barehanded! Once, he went into a factory after the workers had called him to help. They had seen a giant cobra and the whole factory, with about 30 people, had come to a standstill. Without flinching, Sadghuru went and caught the cobra, which was almost 12 feet long! He kept it as a pet with him under his bed in a big jar. One day, while Sadghuru was away, his father went into his room upon hearing some noises. He looked under the bed, saw the giant snake and lost his mind! The snake was living under the bed for almost 3 years. Snakes carry great symbolism for yogis as they represent the kundalini energy in the spine and an aspect of the evolving spirit of the human.

At the age of 25, Sadghuru took an unexpected break from his successful business agenda and hiked up a hill into the wild for no real reason at all. As he sat down to meditate, however, his heart and mind exploded with a timeless realization: everything in the universe is interconnected and everything dissolves into consciousness! The flowers, the village in the distance, and even the bugs and flies were all a part of Sadghuru's spirit. In other words, when one eats a carrot, one is also consuming the microbes from the soil where it grew and therefore becoming the microbes and vice versa. This wasn't just a passing awakening, this was a profound transformation that left him deeply changed. It hit him that all "people are spiritual beings dabbling with the material rather than the reverse" and all of life is simply crying for liberation. What's more, such liberation or self-realization is available and possible for every single person, without question!

After about a year of continuous meditation, Sadhguru decided to teach yoga to share his inner experience. He began conducting yoga classes across Karnataka and Hyderabad, traveling on his motorcycle - a vehicle he has used for spreading the gospel of massive environmental campaigns and causes. Throughout his teachings and activism, Jaggi has become known as a great guru, environmentalist, poet, and mystic.

A nourishing takeaway (inspired by Sadghuru and his "Inner Engineering" courses) invites a journey into yoga for physical, mental, and emotional well-being. Practices such as Hatha Yoga, Upa Yoga, and Shambhavi Mahamudra Kriya, as well as teachings from the Tibetan tradition, such as the Inner Engineering Chakra Activation are all lifelong paths for mind, body and spirit. But even a little bit can help us all!

To start, here is a simple yoga meditation practice that can be experienced today:

1. Begin by finding a comfortable seated position, either on the floor or on a chair. Make sure your spine is straight and your shoulders are relaxed.
2. Close your eyes and take a few deep breaths, allowing yourself to relax and settle into the present moment. Begin by bringing your awareness to your breath. Notice the sensation of the breath as it moves in and out of your body.
3. As you continue to focus on your breath, begin to silently repeat a mantra to yourself. A mantra is a word or phrase that is repeated as a means of focusing the mind. Examples of mantras include "Om," "Peace," or "Love."
4. Continue to focus on your breath and mantra for at least 10-15 minutes, allowing yourself to sink deeper into a state of relaxation and inner stillness.

5. When you are ready to conclude the practice, slowly open your eyes and take a moment to adjust to your surroundings. Take a few deep breaths and gently stretch your body before getting up.

READY FOR GROWTH

It's a long process of figuring out how to live kindly with ourselves. We let disempowering stories, traumas or judgements live rent-free in our heads. We put the past in the future. We take worst-case scenario thinking and negativity bias as reality. To make matters worse, much of our society markets, advertises and sells to our insecurities, nonetheless lacking a higher moral code to the health of its customers. Despite all this rigmarole, the truth remains: nothing can stop a determined soul ready for growth.

For example, a boy was having a hard time on a vision quest. He couldn't shake the memory of when he disappointed his mother and father for not doing something perfectly to their liking and causing double sadness - that of his parents and that of his own for hating himself that he didn't live up to his own or his loved ones expectations. Crying, he ran down to a river near his campsite and was startled to see his own tears in a calm eddy of the water. He whispered to the river:

"Oh, you like to cry too, old river? Is that what you do when you feel sad? I feel like sometimes I get stuck in a bad memory or a ugly thought and can't get free...How do I speak kindly to these parts of me? How do I remember that I'm not just the torrent of thoughts that flow through my head? What if my own opinion and the opinions of others aren't the whole truth? What if there isn't a whole truth and it's just opinions or perspectives? What if you could find something nice to say to me right now? When I become aware of my thoughts, my thoughts become more aware. I am ... finding ... space ... between ... habitual thinking."

This boy is a fictional version of many of us. Perhaps coming into the awakened realization that we have choice in how we think, how we speak to ourselves and ultimately how we live our lives.

LONDRELLE

"I start my mornings with breath and self-analysis.
Giving thanks for life and all of its challenges."

Growing up with a mother who sold crack and a father who was murdered, Londrelle Hall defied the statistics of being another poor eviscerated black boy in America and converted his trauma into spiritual healing and artistic excellence. Born into the projects of Winter Garden, Florida, Londrelle found inspiration through the southern hip-hop movement; a Venn-diagram of swag, musical talent and autobiographical storytelling. But finding his way into becoming a healer and artist was anything but a clear path, it was actually the opposite. After rapping at open mics and writing poetry at bus stops throughout college, he recorded music that went nowhere with zero response from fans or the industry. He even admits to having been forsaken, lost and suicidal at the bottom of a bottom with no end in sight.

Traveling to Atlanta by car with all his belongings and no plan, he arrived to little fanfare and a bunch of bad paying menial jobs. Not too long afterward, however, he witnessed the news of another shooting of another unarmed and innocent black body, Michael Brown. He resolved to do something somehow, grabbed his athletic shoes and started running to clear his head. Next thing he knew it was 7 miles of tireless jogging with an idea that had begun stirring in his heart. After weeks of planning and visioning, he and a friend organized a campaign called #RunforJustice which would travel the 580 mile journey from

Atlanta, Georgia to Ferguson, Missouri, the exact location of the murder of Michael Brown and the 2014 Ferguson civil rights riots.

Londrelle shared further, "At the time, I used running as a tool to help me problem solve and deal with depression and other mental maladies, so my idea was to use this run as a way to positively spread awareness for police brutality and spark some sense of initiative in the youth and the culture as a whole." They were also able to raise about $80,000 for the cause, most of which was donated to the family of the victim.

For the next few months, he continued traveling the United States, holding community gatherings and protests to bring justice for those wrongfully killed at the hands of police officers. Those few months of traveling for social justice sparked a spiritual awakening in him and he paradoxically began to look within for the answers he desperately searched for in the world. He became deeply interested in meditation, studying and practicing eastern spirituality with fervor. His poetry became more occult - drawing inspiration from the words of the Bhagavad Gita, as well as from spiritual teachers such as Paramahansa Yogananda, Ram Dass, and His Divine Grace. A. C. Bhaktivedanta Swami Prabhupāda - and the music he began making followed a similarly mystical trajectory. Since then, his career has exploded into the hearts and minds of millions to help revolutionize the cheesy tropes of a New Age or Wellness industry that needed a makeover. More importantly, Londrelle has opened a world of spirituality to entirely new demographics of people, many of them young black kids, becoming the person he wished for as a child.

A simple takeaway, inspired by Londrelle:

Find a friend or family member to ask to play an affirmation echo game. A mirror will work if you can't find someone else to join. Standing in front of your friend or family member, take 10 deep belly breaths together and then read out loud the following statements - with as much passion and fearlessness as you can possibly muster:

"I love myself without question, condition or concern.
I am happy with my life and my journey.
I have limitless confidence in myself and my greatness.
I can accomplish anything I put my heart and mind to.
I am a true inspiration and a loving presence to all who come across my light.
Accepting myself unconditionally is the best life hack.
Loving myself is as easy as breathing.
I am a blessed and beneficial presence on planet earth.
I walk and breathe in the charmed circle of love's infinite embrace.
I am the peace and love I seek."

A RIDDLE

I am taken from both mine and mind,
and held in a sacred wooden case,
from which I am never released,
and yet I am used by almost every person.
Who am I?

Small as a whisper,
light as a feather,
I am carried on the breeze,
Given away freely,
I bring great pleasure,
Who am I?

I am a powerful force,
yet can be small and insignificant.
I can change lives,
and make the world a better place.
I cost nothing,
but yet I am priceless.
Who am I?

I am a simple thing,
that can lighten a heart,
I require no words,
and I make no sound.
I can be given with ease,
and yet be profound.
Who am I?

*kindness

WIM HOF

"I don't get colds, I go to the cold"

Wim was born the 9th child to working class parents in the Dutch city of Sittard just before Europe's hippie revolution. While everyone else was devoutly Catholic in his family, Wim secretly discovered rare publications on Hinduism and yoga, along with the riveting and mythical *Jonathan Livingston Seagull* book. These uniquely silent discoveries validated an inner calling to go beyond the constraints of this world to live a limitless life. He recalls coveting the knowledge inside these books like sacred treasures in part because he felt horribly lonely in his heart of hearts. How strange to have had an unrelenting spiritual quest as a youth while everyone around you is just trying to go to Sunday school or find a date! Thus, he became a lifelong seeker for the sacred connection between mind, body and soul.

In his early twenties, while walking alone on a freezing morning in Amsterdam, Wim noticed a massive sheet of ice on the canal and like any logical young man with big plans for the day, he stopped everything and jumped into the ice. Was he a thrill-seeker or a madman? Was he a revolutionary freeing himself from the straightjacket of his humdrum existence or an athlete creating a new sport altogether? History tells us that he was all of those. The feeling of that shocking freeze when his body hit the icy water never left him. He later reflected: "The feeling wasn't of cold … it was something like … tremendous good. I was in the water only a minute, but time just slowed down. It felt like ages. The cold is my teacher!"

Wim Hof met his soon-to-be-wife Olaya (also the mother to their 4 children) in the midst of his growing fascination with unusual mind-body experiments. But while his own healing journey started to blossom, his wife descended into a series of bi-polar mental health emergencies, eventually commiting suicide just minutes after kissing their kids goodbye. Wim attributes the challenge of raising his children without their mother as igniting a deep strength needed to move forward, embracing the uncomfortable as a theme throughout his life.

After that fated day of his wife's suicide, it dawned on him that maybe the cold therapy experiments could have benefits for his young kids too. Bringing them into the cold water, Hof witnessed them giggle with immense joy. These innocent experiments gave him the idea to share his personal wellness practices with others, whether or not they were struggling and no matter their age or background. His relentless focus on vitality regimes became a catalyst for bringing this gift to others: journeys into the extremities of nature, along with powerful breath practices, ultimately led to a life of self-kindness and the ability to truly help others. He has hiked Mt Everest in shorts, meditated under ice for hours and... brought millions along with him. As a modern society faced with widespread disease and mental illness, perhaps Wim's rebellious breakthroughs could inspire a mass movement into the discomfort of our own healing and liberation?

Here's a freezingly awesome challenge, inspired by Wim: Can you commit to taking a cold shower (or jumping in cold/freezing water) at least once a day for the next 21 days? The scientific benefits of cold water or ice therapy are now well-documented, but be sure to read as much as you need to feel confident or prepared.

Before taking your cold shower or ice plunge, try 4 X 30 breath rounds of deep inhales and exhales in which you tell yourself the simple affirmation "I am letting go." Each round is concluded with an exhaled breath hold that is held for as long as you are comfortable with, before taking an inhale and holding for at least 15 seconds.

If that's too complicated, try finding one of Wim's books or videos to cross-reference a practice that works for your own mental and physical preparedness to get in the cold. If you can't start with cold water in the shower, end with it, but eventually you should be able to do the breathwork and then a 2-4 minute cold shower for your health and posterity. Let's get wild and strong like the "humanimals" we all are!

SOMETHING AMAZING

There's always something amazing happening in life.

Even when we least think so.

While you're sleeping, your body is breathing you.

When you cry, your tears release endorphins and oxytocin.

A lover you've never met wants to kiss and hug

your pain away.

A shaman in the jungle is reviving a lost plant species

that will provide enough oxygen for you and your whole

family next year.

A friend is making you tea and writing you a letter about how

much you care.

A scientist is solving a major environmental energy crisis.

With ancient symbolism, a mother elephant is stroking

her babies.

An artist is creating a beautiful painting or piece of music that

will ignite a global renaissance of creativity.

A worm is being cultivated that can eat and compost plastic.

A mushroom is being discovered that can heal depression and

clean up toxic waste sites.

Your mother is calling you on the old candlestick telephone to

tell you the secret to true contentment is to smile more, despite

your problems.

Your dad is calling you to apologize, repair and build a new

chapter in your family book.

Your ancestors are calling you all the time, if only you'd listen to your dreams.

Even now, love is as close as your nostrils breathing, as near as a prayer on your lips.

Life is a maze, but it's more than that ... life is amazing.

ADRIENNE MAREE BROWN

"How would I be with the body if there was nothing to fix? There's nothing to fix except for the lens that I'm looking through."

Adrienne Maree Brown (often styled as **adrienne maree brown**) has journeyed a path as a compassionate activist almost her entire life. As a mixed-race child growing up in a military family, she encountered racism and prejudice at an early age and endured the contradictory love-and-punishment parenting style of her southern parents. Despite being labeled as "fat" and undesirable by society's cruel beauty standards, she found solace in radical honesty, decolonized pleasure, and deep scholarship, all serving as a roadmap to her liberation. These experiences molded her perspective and paved the way for her future work, knowing that personal change mirrors systemic change.

While studying African American Studies at Columbia University, Adrienne was deeply affected by the tragedy of the killing of Amadou Diallo by police officers. This event sparked a flame of interest in issues surrounding policing and race that led her from Brooklyn, where she worked with the Harm Reduction Coalition, to Detroit. There, she was warmly welcomed by a supportive community of elders and mentors who offered her their wise counsel and helped her understand the role of cultural organizing in the quest for justice. She fell in love with the city and immersed herself in the local community, where she spent the next twelve years learning from some of the country's most seasoned leaders.

One of Adrienne's greatest influences was the renowned activist and mentor, Grace Lee Boggs. She was blessed to have the opportunity to learn from Grace and participate in many of the initiatives she led. Through her time in Detroit, Adrienne honed her unique style of organizing and gained a reputation for her ability to bring people together to achieve their shared goals. She learned to make a way out of no way and emerged as a confident but kind leader.

Despite her serious political consciousness, Adrienne has since found an unexpected outlet on the internet for her creative side. She has become one of the great queens of memes and mash-up videos, using her wit and humor to curate rare and refined posts that bring laughter or catharsis to her online followers. With her unique blend of comedy and storyweaving, Adrienne has become a beloved figure on the internet, inspiring people from all walks of life.

Adrienne is a much needed voice in the intersectional activism movement, advocating for the dismantling of oppressive systems and the creation of a more just and equitable world. She believes that cultural work plays a critical role in shaping possible futures and is dedicated to harnessing the power of these tools to effect positive change. At the core of her theory of change is the belief that this work must be joyful and nourishing to the body, be it through somatic healing, pleasure-filled lovemaking or just singing with others. Adrienne recognizes that in order to create lasting, systemic change, it is essential to attend to the holistic needs of those who are most affected by oppression and to empower all to reclaim our bodies, desires, and pleasures.

Since Adrienne's work highlights the need for a deeper connection with our bodies, to cultivate a sense of self-love and body positivity, we created this fun little meditative "innercise".

In this meditation, we lie down in a comfortable space. Start to focus on bringing awareness to the body, noticing any sensations, emotions, or thoughts that arise. Take some deep nostril breaths, and while exhaling, imagine releasing any tension, judgment, or negativity towards the body. You can begin to massage, roll around or whatever shakes the tension away.

Now, let's visualize a warm, nurturing light enveloping us, filling us with love, compassion, and self-acceptance. As we continue to breathe, we imagine this light spreading to every part of our body, healing and soothing any pain or discomfort.

Finally, we bring our attention to the sensations of pleasure in our bodies, recognizing the power of our sensuality and the role it plays in cultivating body positivity - it's all welcome and beautiful! Breathe and smile bigly.

Whether we are rolling around on the floor or out in the streets, we can always carry with us this sense of self-love and appreciation for our bodies, knowing that we are enough and deserving of love, just as we are.

THE PELICAN & THE SURFER

A surfer was feeling down, grieving the loss of a close friend. At dawn, he paddled out to the ocean to find comfort and peace. As he sat in the waves, the full moon slipped behind the horizon, trading smiles with the sun as it rose. Just then, he noticed how effortlessly pelicans rode the mist of the waves between the break and the shoreline.

The sight of these ancient creatures in perfect harmony with the waves inspired the surfer to realize that life, too, can be like the waves ˗ sometimes calm, sometimes rough. Or sometimes looking separate from the ocean and sometimes indistinguishable from the ocean. But like the pelicans, we can learn to navigate the ups and downs with grace and find peace in the midst of difficulties or change.

Just then, a bigger swell of waves appeared and the surfer was at the right spot at the right time to catch the best wave of the day. The surfer rode a sweet tube, simultaneously laughing and crying, as if life and death were roaring through the waters at that very moment. Crashing into the sand, the surfer emerged onto the beach as if just baptized. With a newfound appreciation for the ocean and all who share it, the surfer was grateful for the cosmic reminder to live every moment to the fullest.

DARIN OLIEN

"It's so easy for people to blow off 'purpose'. It's a whisper taken over by a megaphone of what the world tells us we should do."

Darin was born two months early, with lungs underdeveloped and a hyperactive thyroid. The doctors were worried about all kinds of things and he was in an incubator for the first three weeks of his life. In a recent interview, he shared that he had a 50-50 chance of surviving, barely prevailing with a resting heart rate of 120 beats per minute for his first few years. It was only through sheer luck and resilient adaptation that he made it through. This remarkable ability to turn life's challenges into life's blessings seems to be a motif throughout Darin's life.

As a 7 year old sitting in his father's beat-up Oldsmobile, Darin asked his father what he wanted to do with his life. Normally, it's the other way around, but in this case, the child's innocence was more far-sighted than the parent's experience. Darin's father wanted to sail and ride motorcycles in freedom, but his alcoholism was more powerful than his dreams.

"Witnessing his struggle impressed upon me the importance of honoring the self." shared Darin in an interview. "I realized that we design our own lives and have the power to move addiction and darkness into the light of love and passion."

After his father died of alcoholism, a deep spark of passion ignited in Darin's life that led to an uncompromising focus on health, wellness and radical joy. With food and culture at the center of his work, he founded Darin's Naturals, a company focused on researching and studying superfoods and healing foods around the planet. Traveling, teaching, authoring books, hosting shows and all the success that followed all came from deep self-commitment to a life without limits.

From overcoming death as an at-risk newborn child to his relationship with his father, Olien's story is one of resilience, adaptability and loving-care. When things fell apart, his attitude created the conditions necessary to evolve and grow rather than fall victim to the crisis of the day. That 7 year old sitting with his father knew more than the vast majority of us: that pain pushes us until vision pulls us. May we all realize such courage!

A nutrilicious experiment, inspired by Darin:

If you can, grab a piece of food to hold. Whether a vegetable, chip or fruit, it doesn't matter. While holding the item in your hand, close your eyes and take a moment to sit in stillness with this object. Begin by thanking it for having traveled from the field to your hands and imagine the incredible journey it took. Now, turn your attention to all the foods that you've ever put into your body and thank the edible universe that sits (and shits!) through you.

In reviewing this edible universe, consider some foods that are truly nourishing. Whole, organic, unprocessed foods such as fruits, vegetables, whole grains, and lean proteins - all providing essential vitamins, minerals, and antioxidants that our bodies need to function at their best. These foods are packed with nutrients that help to protect against chronic diseases and promote overall health. As Dr Mark Hyman says to "Eat the rainbow!"

After reflecting on some facts, ideas or feelings around healthy foods, try to take mental note of any foods that you think may have been harmful. Processed foods, foods high in sugar and unhealthy fats, and foods with added chemicals and preservatives? Foods that did or can lead to weight gain, inflammation, or an increased risk of chronic diseases.

Now, in an imaginary "choose your reality" nutrilicious game, which foods are calling to you now? Are you choosing only for your tongue and taste buds? Do you also choose for the quality of digestion and energy levels after eating? Is there a way to embrace good taste and good nutrition at the same time? Have you considered the impact that your food choices have on our farmer's of the world or on the precarious planet we all share?

As with the quality of your breathing or your water intake, the food you consume has the power to heal and strengthen, or to harm and weaken. As someone wise once said: "Let thy food be thy medicine and thy medicine be thy food." Breathe into the feeling of having already achieved this level of healthy and intentional food experience. Breathe into this type of positive approach for your next meal ... then open your eyes and give the food you're holding a silly hug before eating it mindfully.

INSPIRATION, EXHALATION, LIBERATION

Feel the breath fly in

feel the breath sigh out

Peace is so tough, but it's better than violence

Noise is so loud, let's try silence

Eyes so open, they might be wide shut

The little prince trying kindness

Monk conquering mind's tyrant

Child's helping parent be child again

So serious the news starts smiling

Watch how all events fall & rise to trend

Winds of time pass through bodies pranayam

Somatic forest ocean song within!

Ship's sailing vipassana Buddha

Follow the feeling from here to Bermuda!

Lead your mind like Me, Myself DeRula!

Like Jesus healing Judah!

Strength so deep like lava mountain

Drink of truth like a water fountain

All is inside the heart breath, dear friend

So fresh like smelling herbs from an artist's garden.

LISA NICHOLS

"We are a family, and I love you and believe in you."

Many many years ago, Lisa Nichols found herself in a place that seemed insurmountable. Her bank account held a mere $12, a stark reminder of the struggles she faced as a single mother on public assistance. Rock bottom had become her reality, a place where hope was scarce, and the future looked bleak.

But sometimes, it's in the darkest moments that the seeds of transformation are sown ⋯ as the Christianopoulos couplet reminds us:

"what didn't you do to bury me
but you forgot that I was a seed."

Amid the challenges that life had thrown her way, Lisa refused to surrender to defeat. With unwavering determination, she embarked on a journey to reshape her destiny. She recognized that hitting rock bottom was not the end; it was the catalyst for a new beginning of an even deeper tap root seeded and unstoppable by way of a higher power.

Lisa's journey was not an easy one. As a single mother struggling to make ends meet, she faced numerous hurdles. But within her was a spark of resilience that refused to be extinguished. She devoured self-help books, attended workshops, and listened to motivational tapes. Slowly, she began to uncover the power within her, a power that could turn her breakdown into a breakthrough.

With each challenge she overcame, Lisa's spirit grew stronger. She realized that her experiences were not roadblocks; they were stepping stones towards her dreams. Armed with newfound insights, she started to share her story with others, igniting a spark of hope in those who felt trapped in their own struggles.

Years of hard work, determination, and self-discovery led Lisa Nichols to a remarkable transformation. No longer confined by financial constraints, she rose to become a millionaire entrepreneur. Her journey didn't just end with financial success—she evolved into a best-selling author, a compassionate humanitarian, and a motivational speaker inspiring countless lives.

Today, Lisa Nichols stands as a testament to the power of the human spirit. Through her teachings, she empowers individuals to recognize their untapped potential, just as she did for herself. She helps them discover that breakdowns are not endings, but opportunities for breakthroughs. With every word she speaks, she rekindles the flame of hope, reminding others that their circumstances do not define them.

Meditation on Kindness: Becoming A Seed

Find a quiet space where you can sit comfortably. Close your eyes and take a deep breath, letting go of any tension. As you exhale, release any worries or distractions from your mind.

Step 1: Planting the Seed

Visualize a small, dormant seed in your hand. This seed represents the part of you that has been buried in darkness, overlooked, and forgotten. Hold it gently, acknowledging its presence. Feel the weight of the struggles and challenges that have covered it.

Step 2: The Power of Darkness

Imagine placing the seed in the soil beneath a heavy rock. As you do, recognize that the darkness and weight symbolize the difficulties and hardships you've faced. Just like the seed, you've been in this place of darkness, waiting for a chance to grow and thrive.

Step 3: The Rain of Kindness

Visualize a gentle rain shower beginning to fall around you. Each raindrop is a droplet of kindness, compassion, and love. Feel the raindrops touching the earth, soaking into the soil, and reaching the buried seed. As the rain of kindness seeps in, sense a softening of the darkness and a stirring within the seed.

Step 4: Awakening and Growth

Imagine the seed absorbing the nourishment from the rain of kindness. Slowly, it starts to sprout a tiny shoot. This shoot pushes through the soil, reaching for the light above. This symbolizes the growth that can occur when kindness touches even the darkest corners of our lives.

Step 5: Blossoming

Watch as the shoot continues to grow, unfurling leaves and reaching higher towards the sky. With each inch it grows, visualize your own transformation, healing, and growth. As the shoot blossoms into a vibrant plant, imagine the love and light radiating from it, illuminating the darkness.

Step 6: Reflection and Gratitude

Take a moment to reflect on the journey of the seed, from darkness to growth. Consider the power of kindness in nurturing your own potential for transformation. Feel gratitude for the rain of kindness that has allowed you to heal and thrive.

Step 7: Spreading the Kindness

Now, visualize yourself as a source of rain, a conduit of kindness. See yourself spreading droplets of kindness to others around you, nourishing their seeds of potential. Imagine your kindness touching their lives, helping them find their way through darkness to growth and healing.

Step 8: Return to the Present

Gently bring your awareness back to the present moment. Take a deep breath in, and as you exhale, slowly open your eyes.

As you go about your day, remember the healing power of kindness. Just as a seed can transform with the rain of kindness, so too can our lives. Let your actions be drops of rain that nurture the seeds of potential in yourself and others. Through kindness, we can create a world where even the darkest corners bloom with new life and love.

REBELS

As children, we saw fairies in trees and eternity in the sand.

We saw freedom in chalk and games in a can.

Adventures conjured from our heart & hand.

We saw no limits, no boundaries, no dams.

Imagination saved us, turned the outside in.

Becoming Earthling was tough but so was Martian:

Falling from the stars to remake the world like Skywoman!

Spiritual beings living a weird AI simulation.

Hard but soft, strange but familiar, lost but found again,

Learning to be me or you while interbeing like

Thich Nhat Han.

Rebels but kind, criminals but judges, the band but the fan.

How else could we carry the world without crashing down?

How else could we bring that free light to every coal dark town?

How else could we create our best life in a world of frowns?

DR GABOR MATE'

>"Knowing oneself comes from attending with compassionate curiosity to what is happening within."

Life isn't a collection of events, it's a collection of interpretations. Tragedy can turn to triumph with a courageous and patient perspective. If you don't like your past, change it in your attitude. If you wish something happened differently, make it different today by telling a new story or looking at the event as a catalyst for growth. Often it's just a new pair of glasses or the willingness to face the challenge head on instead of running from it. Often the problem was simply in our attitude or perception. And if there's anything more untrustworthy to the human, it's the mind! It's not to "spiritually bypass" anything in the 3D reality but rather to move through it without getting stuck. Grieve and feel the thing completely but then let that shit go!

That rant is a good segway into the healing trauma work that Dr Gabor Mate has pioneered in his lifelong work. Mate was a Hungarian Jewish infant under the Nazi's and barely survived the genocide. Much of his family were not so lucky and his childhood was marked by the loss of his grandparents and aunt in the Holocaust. His father's trauma from the war - forced labor under the Nazi's brutality - rippled onto a young Gabor and he struggled to come to terms with the horrors of the human condition.

As a youth, after his family had fled to Canada, Mate turned to radical politics and activism (this time against the Vietnam War) to channel his rage and helplessness. Though his fight was on the right side of history, ultimately, he couldn't fight hate with hate and needed a new strategy altogether. He fell in love with a fellow student and began teaching high-school literature but something called him deeper into healing his own wounds and those of the world. It was at that point that Mate decided to pursue a career in medicine and became an M.D. in general family practice. Finally, he had found his calling; he was able to serve those with acute mental or physical trauma to make change, from the inside outward. His 20 + years of service in drug and poverty riddled environments like Vancouver's Downtown Eastside began making headlines when he defended supervised injection sites. Mate strongly believed in the importance of providing harm reduction services to people with substance use disorders, and was willing to speak out and advocate for these services despite horrendous backlash from politicians and the media.

He has pioneered similar unconditional and unconventional healing practices, like that of the sacred Ayahuasca indigenous medicine from the Amazon. He partnered with a Peruvian Shipibo ayahuasquero (traditional shamanic healer) and began leading retreats for addiction treatment, including in a Coast Salish First Nations community that were subject of an observational study by health researchers at the University of British Columbia. The results of the study showed that Mate's claims of therapeutic efficacy were well-founded and that participants had significant improvements in psychological measures and reductions in problematic substance use.

A "letting go" experiment, inspired by Gabor Maté's self-reflection and journaling work. This practice is designed to help individuals gain insight into their thoughts and emotions, and to better understand the underlying causes of their behavior. Journaling encourages individuals to be honest with themselves and to reflect on their experiences, feelings and memories while releasing them to the alchemy of the universe. This can be done by reflecting on whatever comes through your heart, mind and pen in a non-judgmental way.

One way to start this practice is to set aside time each day for self-reflection, and to use prompts or questions to guide your thoughts. Some examples of prompts that Gabor Maté suggests include:

- "What am I feeling right now?"
- "What is the source of this feeling?
- "What are the thoughts and beliefs that are associated with this feeling?"
- "What is the underlying need that is not being met?"
- "How can I best meet this need in a healthy way?"
- "What would help me make peace with my challenging feelings or events in my life?"

It's important to remember that journaling is a personal practice and you can adapt it to your own needs and preferences. It's also important to be consistent with your journaling and, ideally, to make it a part of your morning or bedtime routine. Additionally, you can always visit with a qualified therapist or counselor for guidance and support in your healing journey.

BREATHWORK

Feel your breath as it flows

From nose to mouth, head to toes

From tree to lung, circumference to center

Life is births and deaths, exits and enters

Stage left, this is your story, be heroic

A journey of symbols, a newness so old it

Breathes you ... breathes you inward to lift

Your heart and arms up to the sky

Like an eagle, let your wings fly!

So high you can fall to the stars now!

You're the place to be · from here to mars, wow!

Feeling is healing, body is a river, don't rush,

A strength that only stillness could crush.

It's just you vs yourself in a moonburst,

Whoever you choose wins · no losers.

TARIQ TROTTER / BLACK THOUGHT

"I am a walking affirmation, that imagination
And focus and patience gets you closer to your aspiration
And just 'cause they give you shit don't mean you have
to take it
My words capture greatness, sworn affidavits"

To understand the journey of a modern griot, we can turn our rebellious lens toward the prolific rapper Black Thought, from the legendary hip-hop group, The Roots. Born Tariq Trotter in inner-city Philadelphia, his father was murdered when he was one year-old. His mother struggled with poverty and was also tragically murdered later when Tariq was in high-school. Throughout his upbringing, he dealt with hardships beyond what many experience in a lifetime, dodging arrests for doing graffiti and dealing crack-cocaine.

Understandably, many people would break down and lose faith entirely if they had to face such horrors of poverty and violence. Yet many others, like Fela Kuti or Bob Marley, find a way to turn their trauma into art … and change the world because of it. In other words, those lucky enough to overcome their tragedies, release their past and heal. That's exactly what Black Thought has done, turning his broken heart into a quoted art.

"You often hear people say their history doesn't define them. I've quite honestly chosen to live as more of a vision of the possibilities of the future than as one of a memory of the past."

Even when Tariq was a child facing such turbulence, however, he was a wise soul beyond his years with a propensity for creative genius. He and his close friends would watch parties take place at a recreation center called "The Center" in South Philly, and the MC cyphers that would take place during them. A cipher is a method of encrypting a message to keep its contents secret. In the context of hip-hop, a cipher is a group of rappers who take turns freestyling or rapping over a beat, battling for the most intelligent and stylish delivery. Tariq would climb to the rooftop and look down on the jams, just watching the parties taking place on the basketball courts there. Eventually, building up his confidence and lyrical strategy, he would grab the mic and rap.

When Black Thought met Questlove (the great drummer/producer/DJ) in high-school, he must have found an organic and alchemical collaborator to channel his grief, his spirit and his dreams with. With the novelty and ingenuity of hip-hop at the time, they were true pioneers integrating the blues, jazz, funk and the melting pot of the idiom. The duo founded The Roots and they have gone on to create a library of music, poetry and storytelling over the course of 3 and half decades of recordings, live shows and collaborations.

Black Thought has been successful in film, television, theater and academia. And he's remained a voice for the people - particularly for Black communities around the world - always standing up for what's just and humane.

Feeling up for a creative challenge? Here is a cipher activity inspired by Black Thought that anyone can try at home:

1. Gather a group of friends or family members who are interested in poetry, musical storytelling, rapping and/or freestyling.

2. Choose a beat to rap over. This can be an instrumental from a popular song, a beat from a beat machine or a simple drum or beatbox created by a participant.
3. Form a circle with the participants and start with one person freestyling or rapping. Support the creation with positive energy rather than judgement, even if it doesn't sound amazing at first.
4. After the first person finishes, the next person in the circle takes their turn, building on the previous person's flow and lyrics.
5. Continue the cipher for as long as desired, with each person taking their turn to add their own unique style and lyrics to the mix. Encourage participants to come up with their own rhyming lyrics on the spot and in concert with the drum patterns that play underneath.
6. Allow the group to give positive feedback or kindhearted criticism to each other after the cipher.
7. Above all, have fun and enjoy the experience of creating lyrical music together!

This activity can be fun and a great way to build camaraderie among friends, family or organizations seeking new ways of interacting. It's also a great way to open your own subconscious and repattern neurological pathways simply by way of improvisation and the art of musical storytelling.

~~~~~~

KINDNESS TO OTHERS

~~~~~~

CIRCLE OF KINDNESS

FAITH PRESENCE HUMILITY CREATIVITY LISTENING COMPASSION FORGIVENESS SERVICE VULNERABILITY BREATH GRATITUDE JOY SELF-CARE PATIENCE HUMOR WONDER PRESERVERANCE PERSEVERANCE REST

INNER=SELF MIDDLE=OTHERS OUTER=PLANET

66

KINDNESS TO OTHERS

Participating in - and even witnessing - acts of kindness produces oxytocin, referred to as the 'love hormone' which improves our overall heart-health and lowers blood pressure. Oxytocin also boosts our positivity and inspiration for life, fortifying our confidence to foster empowering relationships in life.

"About half of participants in one study reported that they feel stronger and more energetic after helping others; many also reported feeling calmer and less depressed, with increased feelings of self-worth," according to research done by Christine Carter, UC Berkeley, Greater Good Science Center.

In terms of measuring human joy, a 2010 Harvard Business School survey of happiness in 136 countries found that people who are altruistic—in this case, people who were philanthropists and in general, generous financially -- were happiest overall.

According to research from Emory University, those who are kind to others have our brain's reward & pleasure centers lit, as if the giver were the recipient of the good deed—not the receiver. This is called the "helper's high."

Like medical antidepressants, kindness actually activates the production of serotonin. This feel-good tonic chemical actually heals our wounds, calms us down, and makes us happy.

Human longevity and life expectancy is another factor when measuring the impacts of kindness in everyday life. "People who volunteer tend to experience fewer aches and pains. Giving help to others protects overall health twice as much as aspirin protects against heart disease. People 55 and older who volunteer for two or more organizations have an impressive 44%

lower likelihood of dying early, and that's after sifting out every other contributing factor, including physical health, exercise, gender, habits like smoking, marital status and many more. This is a stronger effect than exercising four times a week or going to church." Christine Carter, Author, "Raising Happiness; In Pursuit of Joyful Kids and Happier Parents."

You remember that old joke: why did the clown donate his salary to a good cause? It was a nice jester!

ALOK

"Learning is the most delightful thing about being alive. So, what I say is, when you mess up is when you're alive, because being alive is about messing up gloriously. And I will fight for that ability to gloriously mess up. What we do then is say, I'm sorry; I'm learning."

Growing up with the dual curse of being a gender non-conforming child and a gifted artist in a conservative Texas town was no easy feat for Alok. How could it be for anyone? Despite the relative acceptance from their family, including their parents, who allowed them to wear their sister's clothes at home, ALOK faced bullying from their predominantly white peers and educational institutions. They describe feeling poetically dissociated from their childhood in order to protect themselves from the pain of ostracization they experienced. Luckily, someone introduced the craft of writing poetry to ALOK and their life was forever changed.

Writing opened a universe of creative expression for ALOK which transcended and alchemized the pangs of a world with limited sight. Writing and creative expression were a liferaft in the storm of bigotry and hatred. Writing and creative expression was a beacon of luminescent dreamscapes with no barriers. In a world of conformist shackles, the art of writing was a simple and accessible pathway to the unbridled freedom they felt inside. And through this writing journey, ALOK discovered a world where they could name their feelings, ideas and stories without fear.

As such, ALOK's early life was about blending together different aesthetics, cultures, and values to create something entirely new. They learned life is an art and the art of life requires collage; taking seemingly disparate elements and combining them to form something greater than the sum of its parts. This approach has become a guiding principle in their life, as they had to create their own narrative and forge their own identity in a world without role models.

A trailblazer of genre-bending and intersectional "artivism", ALOK's unique voice and perspective has resonated with audiences worldwide, establishing them as an underground icon for nonbinary or trans rights and identities. Their works, including "Femme in Public," "Beyond the Gender Binary," and "Your Wound/My Garden," delve into themes of trauma, belonging, and the human condition. The impactful #DeGenderFashion movement that ALOK helped birth has challenged the fashion and beauty industries to create more inclusive products. ALOK is a voice for this generation and calls us all to learn and expand our perspectives to see the human identity as limitless.

Despite all the challenges, ALOK remains grounded and kind, frequently responding to negativity with empathy and compassion. They view the world through a lens of love and offer a prismatic vision that is free from colonial categorization and full of potential. Through their work, ALOK continues to inspire and challenge the world to see reality in a different light and encourages all of us to be our own versions of rebels of kindness.

Here's a writing exercise inspired by ALOK's story:

With the intention to help you tap into your own narrative and emotional landscapes, try to give yourself the space to feel everything you explore within this practice. Don't shy away from your own truth, pain and authenticity.

Begin by finding a quiet place where you won't be disturbed.

Sit comfortably and close your eyes. Take a deep breath in and out, letting go of any tension or distractions.

Visualize yourself as a young person, perhaps similar or different from ALOK, facing challenges and discrimination because of your identity. Can you take yourself back to a specific moment that caused hurt or trauma? How can you write about it with compassion; like a movie where you're the hero and you learn from the lesson rather than get lost in it? Can you lyrically rage or grieve about the traumatic experience while still being forgiving and letting it go with every word you unloose on the page?

Take a few deep breaths and allow yourself to connect with all of your emotions and feelings. Write down whatever comes to mind, without judgment or censorship. Write for 10 minutes, allowing yourself to be completely free in your expression.

When you're finished, read over what you've written. Reflect on any insights or themes that emerged, and take a moment to acknowledge and honor yourself with deep and radical love. Give the page a big and awkward hug!

Take one final deep breath and slowly open your eyes. You can take this writing with you, or leave it behind and burn it in a fireplace, knowing that you've explored a deep part of yourself and allowed yourself to be truly authentic. May it help you grow in freedom and expressiveness.

THE MOST IMPORTANT

The most important word in the dictionary is "others".
The most important thought is "yes".
The most important moment is "now".
The most important thing isn't a thing at all.

The least important word in the dictionary is "hate".
The least important thought is "plastic".
The least important moment is "yesterday".
The least important things are things.

The idea that anything is most or least is also a farce.
That's because words can't convey the love we all have for love.
For example, nothing compares to the kindness felt
from a friend, colleague or family member.
Enemies or villains can also be kind, it's just not how we prefer.

Irony is lost on most of us but true loving-kindness is not.
Our best poems aren't even poems.
Our best non-poems are not ironic,
they're just inspiring forms
of communicating our love for others.

NANDI BUSHELL

"Children, rise up! You can do anything you put your minds to!
You can be a real superhero and save our world!"

Once upon a time, in the land of Nelson Mandela's compassionate revolution, a young girl named Nandi Bushell was born. Though her first breaths were spent in South Africa, Nandi was raised in the UK, identifying as both British and Zulu. One morning while making pancakes, Nandi's father, John, showed her a video of The Beatles' "Hey Jude" and she was instantly captivated by Ringo Starr's drumming skills. With her parents' support, Nandi started taking drumming lessons at the age of six. Despite being a girl in an industry that doesn't treat all so fairly, she has emerged as a rock star's rock star - even at such a young age!

Though watching her perform and play music is awesome in and of itself, Bushell's strong backing for the causes of her generation are why we see her as a rebel of kindness. Nandi's combination of bubbly inspiration with deep care for social & environmental issues is the stuff of heroes. She uses her influence to mobilize action on youth related-challenges from mental health and self-esteem to climate change. She is a strong supporter of the Black Lives Matter movement and has used her platform to raise awareness and fight against racial injustice. She has also been actively involved in breaking the climate media silence and encourages her fans to do their part in taking care of the planet.

Nandi's songs are written, played and recorded herself, showcasing stories about everything from her dad's mental health to her fight to save the earth. She graciously and joyously invites other kids into her journey at every step of the way. Her first single, "The Shadows," highlights the struggles of mental health and encourages people (especially family members) to reach out for help.

> "When your fears have taken their toil
> When the demons have gotten control
> When the shadows won't leave you alone
> I'll be there
> When all your rainbows turned into black
> When the sun has turned its back
> When all of your power bled itself dry
> I'll be there
> For you"

Nandi Bushell is not just a talented musician and lyricist, but also a kind-hearted and compassionate girl who uses her voice and platform to make the world a better place. Her spirit and love for life are truly inspiring, and she is an example of how a single person (no matter their age) can make a huge impact, simply by falling in love with a mode of creative or moral expression.

A fun takeaway from Nandi's story is to challenge ourselves to set a goal in a particular field and work towards it every day, just like she does with her drumming. This could be in academics, work, relationships or any other area where one wants to excel. By consistently putting in the time and effort, anything is possible. Let's anchor this challenge by way of a simple creative visualization.

Close your eyes and dance or shake a bit to get into the rhythm of your body. After you're feeling a bit more relaxed, put your hand to your heart to feel the beat. As you do so, hear the power and mystery that drums inside you! Take a breath and smile with this awareness.

Now, imagine yourself standing in front of a drum set with drumsticks in hand like Nandi. Visualize yourself practicing for hours every day, just as she does. See yourself getting better and better with each passing day, playing faster and more complex beats. Feel the beat of your heart as a metaphor for every day of improvement and imagine the feeling of satisfaction that comes with each new accomplishment. Lastly, see yourself using this growing talent as a tool for helping others!

Repeat this heartbeat drum creative visualization daily, or as often as you like, and watch as your motivation and drive to achieve your goals grows stronger with each repetition. If you vibe with it, try to share this practice with a friend to build accountability as you co-develop.

GODFIDENCE

I did a lot of work to find where I come from

Who what where why when - earth to human

Overcame self-hate, lies, aggression,

Peace was better than being right, my confession

Courage was the map, kindness the mission

Hopped o'r separation, crossed the fence plunge

Into that lake of my own creation,

Hugged myself in the water mirror - wow:

Affirmation fresh in the pray-ground!

Brought my fam, kissed the ground I dance upon

Innercise, exercise, nutrilicious twerking

Service, creativity, meditation

Joy in the big and small things with patience

The healing is in the feeling, be my own best friend

That's why I love me, God - we come round again

What is God if not another word for love?

What is love if not another word for life?

What is life if not another word for chance?

What is chance if not another word for fate?

What is fate if not another word for God?

What is God if not another word for me?

So what does God - or whatever word you use - mean to you?

MARIA RESSA

"Democracy is fragile. You have to fight for every bit, every law, every safeguard, every institution, every story. You must know how dangerous it is to suffer even the tiniest cut. This is why I say to us all: we must hold the line."

In 2021, Maria Ressa, a journalist from the Philippines, was one of two recipients of the Nobel Peace Prize. This recognition was a symbolic landmark for modern society, as the last time a journalist received the award was in 1935! What's even crazier is that the winner back then was a German reporter named Carl von Ossietzky, who couldn't accept the award while imprisoned in a Nazi concentration camp. The Nobel Committee chose to award both Maria and Dmitry Muratov of Russia, for similarly representing conflict-riddled struggles for democracy and peace through journalism. As Mark Twain once said, "History doesn't repeat, but it rhymes."

Born in the Philippines, she moved to the United States in the 1970s with her family as martial law was declared in their homeland. At Princeton University, she studied English with a passion for theater and dance, but it was her return to the Philippines on a Fulbright scholarship that truly shaped her life's mission. As the "People Power Revolution" swept the country, Maria found her calling as a journalist. She reported on the six coup attempts on the Philippine President Corazon Aquino, the impeachment trial of President Joseph Estrada, and other major political events in Southeast Asia. With her relentless pursuit of the truth, she uncovered the growth of terrorist groups in the region, documented their use of social media, and wrote two books on the subject.

Maria returned to ABS-CBN as head of news and current affairs, and in 2012, she founded the website Rappler. The site quickly became a leading source of news in the Philippines, reporting on the extrajudicial killings in Duterte's war on drugs, government corruption, and human rights violations. Her unwavering commitment to truth and justice put her in the crosshairs of the government, and she faced a barrage of lawsuits, harassment, and even arrest warrants. But through it all, she refused to be silenced, and instead used her voice to empower others and fight for what is right. Her struggles are the subject of the documentary "A Thousand Cuts" and her memoir "How to Stand Up to a Dictator," which argues that social media companies have a role in the decline of democracy.

In her Nobel lecture, Maria spoke about an invisible atom bomb that had exploded in the information ecosystem, and how technology platforms had given geopolitical powers a tool to manipulate individuals through psychographic warfare. Only four months after receiving the award, Russia invaded Ukraine, utilizing metanarratives it had been planting online since 2014 when it annexed Crimea. The Russians suppressed information and replaced it with lies, creating fake online accounts, deploying bot armies, and exploiting social media platforms to deceive people. For the American-owned platforms, these divisive activities and controversial half-truths actually generated more engagement and revenue, aligning their financial goals with those of the disinformation operatives.

This marked the first instance of online information warfare tactics that would soon be replicated around the world, from *Duterte* to *Brexit* to *Catalonia* to *Bolsonaro* to *Stop the Steal*. In 2022, Vladimir Putin used the same techniques to invade Ukraine and Maria spoke out on how disinformation, both bottom-up and top-down, could manufacture fake realities.

In the same year, the Philippines held its elections to choose a successor to President Duterte. The race came down to two candidates, opposition leader Leni Robredo and Ferdinand Marcos Jr., son of the former dictator Ferdinand Marcos. On election day, Marcos Jr. took an early lead and never lost it. The election proved to be a showcase for the impact of disinformation and relentless obfuscation operations on social media, which transformed Marcos from a pariah into a hero. Disinformation networks from not only the Philippines, but also from other countries, including China, helped alter history. Maria has repeatedly emphasized the importance of integrity in elections and facts. She believes that whoever wins the election not only determines the future but also shapes the past. Tragically, in this election, "facts were lost, history was lost, and Marcos won".

Maria is lucky compared to those who are in hiding, in exile, or in jail. She believes that the only defense a journalist has is to shed light on the truth and expose lies. Many others are persecuted in the shadows and have neither exposure nor support under governments that act with impunity, with technology serving as their accomplice. Maria believes that the aftermath of this silent nuclear holocaust in the information ecosystem must be addressed in the same way that the world addressed the aftermath of World War II. She envisions a world that is more compassionate, equal, and sustainable, safe from fascists and tyrants.

Maria's journey is not just about her, but also about the reader. Democracy is extremely fragile and must be protected through every law, safeguard, institution, and story. People must be aware of the danger of even the slightest cuts to democracy. Maria and her team ask themselves and others every day, "What are you willing to sacrifice for the truth?"

Inspired by Maria's courageous mission, we've put together a few challenges to explore in your own life as you reflect on her journey and message:

1. Research and write an article on a social issue in your community. Share that with a local school or relevant learning group that seeks to explore the importance of compassion or fairness in human societies.
2. Contact a local journalist or media outlet and ask to shadow them for a day to learn more about their work.
3. Host a community event to educate people on the importance of media literacy and critical thinking.
4. Write a letter to a local politician or government official, highlighting a specific issue that needs attention and action.
5. Start a social media campaign to promote truth, justice, and kindness in your community.

A EULOGY TO READ WHEN I DIE

Oh soul, who birthed and died naked bare,
A child of God, a parent of truth and dare.
A helper and artivist, with an art of gold,
A lover of life, the earth, and all that's bold.

Your spirit soars like a bird in flight,
With passion and purpose, a guiding light.
You touched millions of lives and healed hearts with ease,
A comedian for kindness, a warrior for peace.

You lived a life filled with wonder and joy,
And oh what a life it was, full of grace and poise.
With a heart full of love, you stood up for all,
A ring for interdependence, everyone on that telephone call.

Though you made mistakes and lost the truth once or twice
You always knew down comes up, peanut butter loves jelly,
beans do rice.
You always found a way to land on your feet, pray and play.
Dancing the 7 seas, searching for truth inside,
dreaming awake.

You left behind memories that will never fade,
Flowers mandalas, song circles, improv games, muffins made.

So don't ever say goodbye cuz love energy will always remain,
In the hearts of all who knew you, forever ingrained.

Rest now, dear soul, in the arms of the divine,
Grab a meal with kindred spirits in a soul food restaurant dine.
Take off your skin clothes, let go of all old identities
You're source, as you've always been, God's amenities.

STEPHEN CURRY

"Success is not an accident, success is actually a choice."

Behind the celebrity, there was blood, sweat and tears. Behind the champagne parties, there were early mornings. Behind the cover stories, there were sprained ankles and calloused hands. Behind the effortless game-winning basket, there were a thousand missed shots per day. Behind the championship, there were 10,000 failures and 10,000 dejections. Behind the veil of individualized super-human superstardom, there was a team built on unity, integrity and kindness. An icon of such success is not solely a result of their own making, but rather the culmination of inspiration and guidance from those who came before them, and their ability to convert this inspiration into service to the larger community and team they are a part of.

When Stephen Curry was 9 years old, and the youngest player on his team, he missed two game-tying free throws and thought the world had just ended! This was a national championship game and he missed both the free throw to tie the game and the next one as well. So by missing those two free throws, they lost the game. Luckily, given the unconditional love his parents offered him, he witnessed his emotions fly by like seconds on the shot clock and found a deeper truth that failure isn't the end of the world after all.

Growing up in a basketball family, Steph faced the odds of achieving his dream of becoming a professional basketball player. Despite being told he was "too short and skinny," he never gave up and worked tirelessly to prove his greatness to himself and the naysayers. He learned the importance of hard work, determination, and humility from his father, Dell Curry, a former professional basketball player himself.

But Steph's greatness extends way beyond the court. He, along with his wife, Ayesha, have been actively involved in serving their community through their family foundation, providing healthy food and literacy programs to those in need. Hundreds of thousands of children across the world have been fed nutritious food and read important books because of Steph's kind-hearted character.

A true champion is not just measured by their achievements on the field but also by their integrity, kindness, and service to others. Steph Curry is a shining example of this, and his story serves as a reminder that anything is possible with hard work, dedication, and a good heart. If only the world were more supportive of all the little Steph Curry's out there, we might be able to see the unlimited potential in every child and help them fulfill their dreams, not only for themselves but for the greater community and planet at large.

Let's try a creative experiment inspired by Steph's story:

1. Grab a piece of paper and bag of crayons or colored pencils or just a pen, whatever you have.
2. Find a quiet, comfortable place to sit. Close your eyes and take a few deep belly breaths.
3. Now, envision a vision for excellence in all aspects of your life, not just in your professional or career pursuits, but also in how you treat others and give back to your community. This can be achieved by maintaining a good

heart and a humble attitude toward those in your orbit or whatever you feel is most excellent to you.

4. Visualize yourself on the basketball court being coached by Steph! See you both working hard, practicing, and pushing your mind & body to the limits. Feel the determination and dedication he brings to the game of life!

5. As you continue to breathe deeply, say to yourself: "I have the determination, dedication and good heart to achieve these goals."

6. Take a deep breath in, and as you exhale, let go of any doubts or fears you may have about achieving these goals.

7. Continue to breathe deeply and open your eyes, grab the drawing instrument and begin to draw any symbol, image or statement about your commitment to yourself and the world.

8. When you're ready, hang your drawing in a prominent place you will see everyday as a reminder of your beautiful life vision!

FRIENDLY UNIVERSE

There we human raced and cursed,

arguing over whose car wrecked worse

While the sun watched us in a luminous dress.

It was my pain vs yours, road of opposites, in a star lit hearse.

I scream at death, while you sing for life,

calling pain just a cause for the caterpillar's burst.

I read the New York Times, you read the Akashic records first.

I want to escape while you just want a home,

even if our hair's a mess.

I want politics, you just want love undressed:

"Like Rumi said, beyond wrong or right is a field of bless!"

We agree to take a taxi together, to put this to the test.

Let's go to that field, address the whole congress:

You say, "Don't we live in a friendly team universe?"

I say, "Who's taking the limousine service?"

You say ...

To join the ride, you must let go of the stress,

Try 90 prayers of forgiveness,

per mile, till you reach Mt. Kindness!

If this road of ignorance isn't bliss,

then innocence just needs more experience;

Attitude is destiny, be destined for greatness!

And wisdom honors everything from landmarks to pits.

Nothing isn't beautiful, no signs are clueless.

If we want the trip to freedom, it's massive:

Seeing love in all, even in the wackness,

Spreading love, even for the fascists.

From bus to train to plane to hovercrafter,

Giving fair rides to all, it's the science of laughter.

This journey reminds me: life's not all bad shit!

Children remind me we can transport to a new age, Ecozoic.

A swim in a clean ocean, a forested backflip,

Nature reminds me, it's all just energetics!

We can either be right or be in relationship.

The challenge of sharing the road is this:

whether we can live with respect to difference!

We come to realize that yes ...

It's our friend, the entire earth;

the road, the universe.

MILA KUNIS

"You've got to base your career on something other than being FHM's top 100 number one girl. Your looks are going to die out, and then what's going to be left?"

Kids growing up in Jewish families often learn that helping others is a high form of human intelligence and should be aspired to as often as prayer. This belief is rooted in the traditional Jewish concept of tzedakah, which translates to "justice" or "righteousness." Tzedakah is often understood as the obligation to perform acts of charity and to help others in need. In Jewish teachings, tzedakah is considered to be one of the most important commandments, and it is often equated with prayer in terms of its importance.

Did such wisdom reach the heart of young Mila in the 1990's Ukraine? We might only assume it did since - despite the tide of antisemitism and religious intolerance in the Soviet Union - her family raised her with the wisdom of her ancestors. She immigrated to the United States in 1st grade. On her second day in Los Angeles, Kunis was enrolled at Rosewood Elementary School, not knowing a word of English.

She later recounted: "I blocked out second grade completely. I have no recollection of it. I always talk to my mom and my grandma about it. It was because I cried every day. I didn't understand the culture. I didn't understand the people. I didn't understand the language. My first sentence of my essay to get into college was like, 'Imagine being blind and deaf at age seven.'

And that's kind of what it felt like moving to the States." No hardship could stop her, however, because her creativity and focus on learning helped transcend the trials of her heritage and culture clashing.

The struggle ultimately proved successful after landing many acting gigs and one that introduced her to her lifelong sweetheart, Ashton Kutcher. In a world of fake gestures and pretend help, their journey into humanitarian aid and charity work has delivered remarkable impact. Time is quickly proving that she's landed in the great tradition of other humanitarian celebrities like Aubrey Hepburn or Barbara Streisand. And her husband only amplifies the impact! If that little girl who went through all those trials could only fast-forward 25 years, she might smile and do it all over again.

A cross-cultural invitation, inspired by Mila:

1. Start by authentically learning about a different culture or community that might be calling for support somehow and that you've had some interaction with, so as not to make it too one-dimensional. Research and connect with the history, traditions, and challenges that they may have faced.
2. If you're moved, find a way to get involved and make a difference. This could be through volunteering, donating to a relevant charity, or simply having a conversation with someone from that community to learn more about their experiences.
3. Reflect on how you can incorporate the lessons you've learned into your own life. Consider ways to be more inclusive and understanding of people who may be different from yourself.
4. Share your experience with others and inspire them to take the challenge too. Encourage them to learn about a

different culture or community and to find ways to make a difference.

5. As a final step, after a month or so, evaluate how you feel after doing this challenge, how your perspectives changed and how you can keep this perspective in your daily life.

This invitation can help you understand the struggles of others, open to the ways you're more similar than not, and inspire you to take action in the world, just like Mila did.

KINDNESS IS A BOOMERANG

Kindness is a boomerang,
Thrown with a soothing fling,
Comes back doubled, whirling,
Like a dervish praying
or a force multiplying,
Like a karmic blessing
Or a gift that keeps giving.
It's a smile on a stranger's face,
A child you helped turn failure to grace
It's a frown you turned upside down,
It's the warm embrace, #huglife now!
A pep talk hotline for the lonely town.
It's the best thing on the "train of wow".

A kind act, a joy imparted
Lifts the spirit, warms the heart with
Honey to balance bitter tart bits
Of life, reverse-kinja-near it
from end to start gifts
Us all with a purpose to care, it's cathartic
To look for ways to help,
a surprise bouquet or homemade garlands.
In every act, whether great or small
Carries the power to heal and mend us all.

So let our words be soft and sweet,

For tomorrow they may come for a receipt.

A simple smile, a listening ear

Can chase away a friends' fear.

A helping hand, a willing mind,

Can go a long way like a big sigh.

In a world where sorrows thrive,

A bit of kindness brings us back to life.

PAUL FARMER

"If access to health care is considered a human right, who is considered human enough to have that right?"

Not always known as "the man who would cure the world," a young boy named Paul grew up poor, moving between an old mobile home (a transformed old school bus) and a commercial fishing boat that his father captained through the Gulf Of Mexico. His father was a "free spirit," and anchored their houseboat in a primitive bayou called Jenkins Creek where the family bathed and fetched drinking water by hand in jugs. Farmer's parents read weighty literature to their children, motivating them to learn as much as possible about the cosmos and all of humanity. One summer, Farmer's family worked with Haitian migrant workers picking citrus fruit, which was Farmer's first important connection, out of many, with Haitian people. This unique childhood of experiential learning is one of many things that helped him be a tireless ambassador of social justice and care for the poor.

As a dedicated and focused student, Paul used his passion for learning to take him all over the world, with staggering impact. Starting in Paris, living abroad while still a student attending Duke (with a Bachelor of Arts in medical anthropology,) Paul studied the work of Rudolf Virchow, a 19th century German physician and scientist who developed public health medicine. His learnings were further deepened by the political atmosphere of the time, with revolutions breaking out across Central America (Nicaraguan Revolution, Salvadoran Civil War, and

Guatemalan Civil War), and the rise of liberation theology which the Catholic clergy used to defy authoritarianism in the region. Such theology focused on the "preferential option for the poor," which passionately argued that the physical and spiritual wellbeing of the poor are a crucial part of the word of God. To many Christians, "liberation theology" calls on the moral courage to focus on their primary obligation in helping the least fortunate. In other words, we are only as strong as our weakest link.

Farmer later became involved with migrant labor camps near his school campus, and there he met Sister Juliana DeWolf. Sister Juliana was working with the United Farm Workers, seeking to ease the subhuman conditions of the tobacco laborers. Through this experience, Farmer befriended many of the Haitian farm workers, and listened to their life stories, a catalyst for his learning Creole and Haiti's history. He started working with villages in Haiti's Central Plateau to help incorporate modern health care practices in their communities, writing more than 100 scholarly papers and several books. Whether founding "Partners In Health" or pioneering community-based treatment strategies that deliver high quality health in resource-poor settings, Farmer changed the landscape of medicine with a dose of kindness.

A compassion meditation, inspired by Paul:

1. Find a quiet, comfortable place to sit. Close your eyes and take a few deep breaths into the deepest part of your heart.
2. Begin by focusing on yourself and bringing to mind a feeling of compassion and love for yourself. Repeat to yourself: "May I be happy, may I be healthy, may I be safe, may I be at ease."
3. Gradually expand your focus to loved ones and friends, wishing them the same: "May [name of loved one] be

happy, may [name of loved one] be healthy, may [name of loved one] be safe, may [name of loved one] be at ease."

4. Continue to expand your focus to include acquaintances, people in your community, and eventually all beings, repeating the same phrases: "May all beings be happy, may all beings be healthy, may all beings be safe, may all beings be at ease."

5. As you focus on each group of people, imagine yourself sending them healing energy and compassion. See them surrounded by light and free from pain and suffering.

6. As you continue to focus on each group, take a deep breath in, and as you exhale, let go of any feelings of judgment, anger or hatred. Stay focused on the feeling of compassion and love for a few more minutes.

7. When you're ready, slowly open your eyes, feeling refreshed and motivated to help others in need.

This meditation can also be done by visualizing a person or a group of people, who are in dire need, and sending them your love, healing energy, and well-wishes.

MORAL COURAGE

Sweet Jesus, Sweet Idris, when did the world invent sin?

Was it the loss of village life and a course correction?

It seems like life has become a giant confession

From scandal to cancel to yesterday's sexting

Now everything is canceled because mistakes are so wretched

Like being you with enough guilt to last 13 moon metrics

A criminal record doesn't compare to the Akashic records

Thankfully, when we lose, we never lose the lesson

From Poland's old ghettos, forgiven but not forgetting

With only 10% of an entire people surviving,

Try turning pain into blessings!

A holocaust arrested turned to Hollywood repping,

But only when moral courage stayed centered.

Two wolves inside us all; it's which one is fed more or lessoned?

Do we choose judgement or acceptance?

Since history is a story of what's unwritten,

Where is the invisible pen for this peaceful conscription?

These are the battles of violence vs communication

Duels between enemy and self-liberation

Trash vs compost. Damnation vs absolution.

JUDY HEUMAN

"One cause of discrimination – in any group – is the lack of breaking bread together, not being together and misinformation ... ultimately if people were living in the same communities and working together, we'd have more of a sense of responsibility to each other."

Joseph Campbell said that "where you stumble, there lies your treasure" and this is especially true for those who grow up with systemic stumbling blocks in the way. Despite the horrific obstacle of contracting polio at age 2 (leaving her unable to walk from a young age), Judy refused to let her physical limitations define her. Heumann's journey is one of perseverance, determination and the kindness to fight for others with "good trouble".

Growing up in Brooklyn, she was surrounded by the unwavering love and support of her parents, German Jewish immigrants who had lost family in the Holocaust. They knew that their daughter deserved an education, but in a world that had little room for disability, they were met with vapid resistance and discrimination. On the first day of school, the principal had the nerve to call Judy a fire hazard and physically block her from entering the building. There were no civil rights or liberties for disabled peoples at the time and America was as mean as it was paradoxical in its "liberty and justice for all" credo. Luckily, her mother, a fierce and unyielding woman dubbed "Mighty Mite" by her husband, was not one to accept "no" for an answer. They fought for Judy's right to learn and won.

As an adult, Heumann picked up where her mother left off and continued to fight for her rights and the rights of others with disabilities. She took on the New York Board of Education and won, becoming a teacher. She shut down traffic in Manhattan, stood up for her right to a seat on an airplane, and even launched a sit-in at a federal building in San Francisco (fed lunches by the Black Panthers) to force Nixon to sign the historic Rehabilitation Act.

Susan Mizner, director of the American Civil Liberties Union's Disability Rights Program, calls Heumann "the mother of the disability rights movement in so many ways" — an activist "who doesn't take crap, never has." Through her tireless efforts and relentless spirit, she played a crucial role in the passing of the Americans with Disabilities Act and continues to be a powerful advocate for the rights of people with disabilities. Heumann's story is a shining example of the power of the human spirit to overcome adversity and effect real change in the world.

A radical acceptance practice, inspired by Judy: find a comfortable seated position, close your eyes and take a deep breath in through your nose and out through your mouth.

Focus on your lengthening breath, and as you inhale, imagine yourself filling up with a sense of openness and curiosity. As you exhale, imagine yourself releasing any judgments or preconceptions you may have about yourself or others at this moment.

As you continue to breathe, bring to mind a person from a background very different from yours, perhaps with a disability.

It could be someone you know or someone you've never met. Imagine this person in your mind's eye, and see them as they are, with all their unique qualities, experiences, and perspectives.

Now, silently repeat the following phrase to yourself: "May you be happy, may you be healthy, may you be safe, may you be at ease." Repeat this phrase as many times as you like, sending loving-kindness and well-wishes to this person.

As you continue to repeat this phrase, imagine yourself becoming more open and accepting of this person, and all people from different backgrounds. Imagine yourself seeing them not as different from you, but as fellow human beings, with powerful stories and ideas that can be tremendous gifts for the world. See their gifts or services being received and contributing to the well-being of all.

When you're ready, take one more deep breath in and out, and gently open your eyes. Remember that this practice of mindfulness and loving-kindness can be done anytime, and can help you to cultivate a more open and accepting attitude towards people from different backgrounds or those you might not currently understand.

SEEDS OF CONSCIOUSNESS

A tree is known by its fruits;
a friend is known for their patience.
Good acts are never lost;
grow flowers and smell the fragrance!
When we plant love, we heal all the nations!
Unlearn our warring and all of this hatred:
Even in the ghetto, life is sacred,
This future is now, this future is ancient.

Take solace in the being & doing, see the two in the one.
A perspective of sunglasses, but not only for the sun,
to avoid being blinded by delusions of grandeur;
fame & riches serve so few, while causing so many to suffer.
Instead, empower the soul to the light,
so that we may cherish these fleeting moments of life.
Let us plant the seeds of consciousness,
cultivate the soil of abundance and harvest happiness.
Sharing our bounty is one of the joys of kindness.

IRMELA MENSAH-SCHRAMM

"Simply because looking away approves and encourages the authors [of hate]. I believe that he who keeps silent and looks away becomes an accomplice."

Cultural change precipitates political change and one courageous woman in Germany found a calling in making sure her country's cultural expression reflects the values of healing, pluralism and justice. For more than 30 years Irmela has painted over neo-Nazi graffiti and propaganda in Germany. In her 70s, the retired teacher who lives in a humble flat in Berlin, is proud to have defaced more than 100,000 manifestations of far-right sentiments, extremism or violence.

She began doing this work in 1986 after seeing a sticker at a bus stop near her home in Berlin wrongly calling for the release of Nazi war criminal Rudolf Hess. Shocked when she returned and found that no one had removed it, she decided to scrape it away with her keychain. After this incident, she began to notice neo-Nazi and right-wing extremist graffiti wherever she went, and resolved to make removing it a part of her daily routine.

As of 2021, she had removed at least 90,000 stickers, with many of these preserved in binders for posterity, and effaced at least 10,000 spray-painted messages or symbols. According to the *New York Times*, "Over her 30 years of scraping, dissolving and painting over far-right slogans, she estimates she has been assaulted three or four times. But, she said, she has also been hugged by strangers and thanked." Benevolent rebels know no bounds for their moral center and willingness to stick their necks out of the embetterment of others; the world is a better place because of them.

A fun challenge for you, inspired by Irmela: Try another benevolent prank! A benevolent prank is a playful and harmless prank that is meant to bring joy and laughter to others. Here are a few examples for you to try below.

1. "Flower Bombing": Leave a bouquet of flowers on someone's doorstep or car, ring the doorbell or knock on the window and run away, leaving the person to find the surprise flowers.

2. "Positive Graffiti": Create positive messages on post-its and stick them on mirrors, windows, or any other public place, spreading positivity and inspiration for people to find.

3. "Rebel act of kindness": Leave a thoughtful gift or a creative note of gratitude for a stranger, in a place where they will find it unexpectedly.

4. "Pay it forward": Pay for someone's coffee or meal in a restaurant, and ask the server to deliver the message "pay it forward" to the next person in line, encouraging them to do the same.

5. "Chalk the walk": Use colorful chalks to draw positive messages, quotes, or drawings on the sidewalks, driveways, and other public places in your neighborhood.

Remember, the key is to make sure that the prank is not offensive or harmful, and that it is meant to bring joy and positivity to others.

EXCEPT LOVE

Life is full of stories that show how hard it can be to choose love over hate. A few thousand years ago, when Jesus was spitting proverbial lyrics on the rap song of history, he shared the parable of the good Samaritan. At the time, Jews and Samaritans (another Abrahamic ethnoreligious group) hated each other for no good reason. One day, a Jew was traveling down the perilous road from Jerusalem to Jericho, when he was attacked by robbers. He was beaten half-dead and stripped of all possessions.

By chance, a Samaritan priest was passing by and was moved to care for him with an almost superhuman level of kindness. He bound up his wounds, poured healing oils and then carried him to an inn where he could be cared for. Not only that, but he gave the innkeeper money to care for the Jew, no questions asked. Jesus then asked his listeners: "Now which of these three do you think seemed to be a neighbor to him who fell among the robbers?" Jesus paused for effect, "He who showed mercy on him!"

This famous story leads to the question of how to overcome our baser tribal instincts of "othering" and learning to care for those who are in need. It also demonstrates how easy it's been for humans to hate or bias against those who are different if we're not careful. "Negativity bias" is a viable culprit inside the human mind. Agriculture might have pushed humans into a culture of amassing and hoarding more than what we need and thus creating armies or power systems of hate to sustain this greed. Nature itself might be to blame since much of the natural world fights for food or ostracizes those who can't keep up with the pace of survival.

But why have we gone to such lengths to uphold the sheer ugliness of hatred as a species when we have the choice to live in a different way? Why are our most famous movies, songs and books filled with abhorrent villains and terrible people doing terribly hateful things and why are those the titles that get the big budgets or click-bait? Politics is rife with the h-word, seemingly thriving off its pathetic race to the bottom of the moral mosh-pit. But don't we all intuitively know that no matter the situation, hate shrinks the brain and personality while destroying our ability to resolve the very issue we hated in the first place.

So, what are the remedies to this global malady? Some say it's the disease of "othering" or "victimizing" that need deep therapies like nonviolent communication. Some say it's about education and teaching healthy ways of processing anger, grief or problems. Some even say it's just human nature to rage, hate and war for what you wish you had or don't wish you have now. Perhaps it's all of this. Perhaps it's none. Perhaps we need to talk about it more so that it's less confusing, controlling or overwhelming. Perhaps we just need more skills and tools to work through this entrenched bias or hatred of those who are different. Perhaps a lovelier world is awaiting us all but we just don't see it yet?

SCHONE MALLIET

> "Socializing the process from never-ever to being good at it, makes all the difference."

Back in the day, a young BIPOC military brat and budding businessman looked around to find others his age, or those from his cultural background, at the country clubs or outdoor sports venues he loved to frequent. Most would never go because they were too intimidated to visit such cultures of racism. Being someone who always sought to better the lives of others through better business, Malliet began exploring ways of creating a more compassionate and kind outdoor sporting environment for all. Data also shows that diversity, kindness and inclusion benefits every other aspect of organizational success as well.

To serve that mission, Schone co-founded the *National Winter Sports Education Foundation* to encourage teens, especially teens of color, to get over the fear that was once associated with country clubs of the 50s and 60s and venture outside their limitations to learn to ski. He's helped thousands of kids overcome these systemic and generational obstacles simply by giving them a platform and strategic support. Malliet also founded the *National Winter Activity Center*, the United States' first 501(c)(3) nonprofit facility/outdoor winter environment dedicated to improving the lives of youth through winter activity. Through its program "Elev8," the Center provides instruction, healthy meals, equipment, and role model/mentoring. Through partnerships with YMCAs, Boys &

Girls Clubs, Schools, and other youth-serving agencies, the Center serves thousands of kids.

Improvements in health and well-being are achieved through a combination of regular exercise, a nutritious diet, and personal growth. By participating in these programs, individuals are able to improve their physical and mental well-being, leading to positive changes in their lives, including a brighter outlook. Through mastering snow sports and life skills, their participants are empowered to explore new opportunities in academia, personal development, and athletics.

How about a somatic leadership habit to develop? Try to create a simple wellness program for your family or community that incorporates exercise, nutrition, and personal development! The program could involve the following components:

1. Exercise! Engage in one moderate to vigorous activity everyday such as sports, hiking, or running. The program could also include fitness classes, such as yoga or strength training, to provide variety and cater to different fitness levels.
2. Nutrition! Educate yourselves on healthy eating and meal planning. Find a friend, book, nutritionist and/or dietitian for personalized guidance.
3. Personal Development! Engage in activities that promote self-awareness, self-care and personal growth. These could include workshops, journaling, and mentorship.
4. Goal Setting! Set individual goals related to physical and mental well-being, and work towards achieving them everyday. This also works best when you include regular check-ins and progress evaluations to help stay on track.

This program could be tailored to different age groups, and could also be organized in a community center, a school or a sports club.

PAST, FUTURE & PRESENT

Past

I'll never let it go ... I can't believe they did that to me!

Future

Even worse is what they're planning to do next week ... it's going to be a total disaster! Imagine all the things that could go wrong!

Past

Well, that's exactly what happened last time so it's 100% going to happen again!

Future

Totally, history doesn't repeat but it does rhyme ...

Present

Take a big deep breath. When have you ever lived in anything other than the present? Living in the present will give you clarity on past mistakes without harboring blame, guilt or animosity. Living in the present will also give you peace, intention and intelligence for how to best handle the future. Breathe into right now and live with greater skill and resilience.

CLINTON KANU

"God is helping me help those suffering from injustice."

Arrested for a crime he did not commit and sentenced to death at age 27, Clinton has the spirit of a thousand dancing elephants. Nearly 30 years after being arrested, he has been exonerated and finally set free! Despite multiple suicide attempts in prison in a horrific penitentiary system, he authentically discovered the voice of God and studied counseling, therapy and Christianity; even becoming a reverend inside his prison academy. Now 56 years old, he is working towards prison reform in Nigeria because the human rights abuses are so treacherous. His mission is to improve life for inmates and to establish a nonprofit that will help people transition to a better life after incarceration.

Nigeria's criminal justice system is rife with corruption. Judges have been suspended for misconduct and caught accepting bribes. Excessive delays compound the problems, with enormous backlogs of stagnant legal cases. Nearly 70 percent of the country's approximately 74,000 prison inmates are awaiting trial. The long waits contribute to overcrowded prisons. The maximum-security prison in Port Harcourt, where Kanu was transferred after he was sentenced in 2005, held more than 4,000 inmates last year, although it was built for 804, according to figures from the federal government.

"And the Lord said, 'I have surely seen the affliction of my people which are in Egypt,'" he recites in a gentle voice, eyes moving over the words. In the room's stuffy heat, beads of sweat settle in the dip above his lip. "'I have heard their cry.'" Now a leading voice in the Nigerian faith community, Kanu uses his spirit as a catalyst to share this story with the world. Nothing on earth can stop a devoted heart to a cause that that heart truly believes in.

Can we sit with an appreciation of freedom? Even if we're in the experience of confinement, seeking a deeper meaning or metaphysical understanding can bring a sense of peace beyond all conditions. So ... let's try to contemplate the idea that true freedom comes from within, and that even in the most restrictive of physical or mental conditions, the ability to find inner freedom through spiritual practice or connection to a higher power can provide a sense of liberation. Additionally, the idea that Spirit (or whatever you name it) is present in all places, including prison, can bring comfort and solace.

Anchored by the breath, bring your attention to anywhere in the body that feels peaceful and free from pain. Deep breaths in and hard breaths out, all while letting go of feelings of anger, frustration or hopelessness. Try to cultivate feelings of gratitude and forgiveness, no matter how hard it may be!

As you've calmed down the nervous system, envision a peaceful place, such as a beach or a forest, and bring that imagery into the mind's eye during this meditation. Allow an angel (or ancestor) to sit with you in that special spot and tell you all the wisdom they know. Allow their kindness and love to pervade throughout your breathing.

Remember that this practice is a reminder that our inner world is where true freedom resides. But it may take time to see the benefits so don't get discouraged if you're struggling with any of this. Start with small sessions and gradually increase the time. It may also help to join a meditation group or take a class to learn more about different approaches and to connect with others who are also seeking inner peace and freedom.

A NEW SYSTEM

"The system" is broken, designed to deceive,
A few have it all, while most can't even breathe
As if life is just a stock market traded for grief.
But hand in hand, we can start to conceive,
Of a new myth, both ancient and modern,
An inward journey, that's unique but common.
Beloved by all, alchemical in essence,
A holiday every day, it's past time for presence,
Gifting 100% of humanity, large and small.
With generosity's charm, dazzle and enthrall.
Nature's alarm rings, as purpose takes action,
Emerging to seed, a deeper satisfaction.
Built upon the present moment, with love as the key,
What's opposite of broken, a self-made society free.
Find us in the poet's forest or magi's ocean.
In every breath we take, in every new notion,
Born from love, a new system is formed,
With artistic genius, a world adorned!

LADY GAGA

"It's always wrong to hate, but it's never wrong to love."

Gaga was a natural musician from a young age, able to sing and play the piano with ease. But things weren't always easy for her in other areas of her life, especially while studying at the Convent of the Sacred Heart school. Even at 11 years old, Gaga was very different from the other girls. She was much smaller and plumper than the rest, with large front teeth that added insult to injury. And because of her unique appearance and eccentric habits, she was bullied very badly by her classmates.

When she was 19, she was raped and dropped on a street corner, pregnant and vomiting. With PTSD so bad it almost killed her, she's spent her life struggling to heal this terrible encounter. A few years later, she developed fibromyalgia, a chronic illness so intense that it has led to severe pain and tour cancellations throughout her career.

Despite these traumatic and humbling experiences, or perhaps because of them, Gaga has grown into a passionate advocate for mental health and the power of kindness in reimagining our world altogether. She uses her influence to promote holistic health among young people by making kindness cool again, validating the emotions of young people, and eliminating the stigma surrounding mental health.

This theory of change has far reaching implications. In a recent survey by Indeed and the Born This Way Foundation found that "soft skills", such as kindness, empathy and mental health, are particularly important to Gen Z and millennial workers. They want to work for employers that model these qualities and prioritize the mental well-being of their employees. In a time when many employees are leaving toxic corporate cultures, companies that take steps to understand why employees are leaving and take meaningful action to retain them can gain a competitive edge. By reading the writing on the wall, rather than staying blind to what workers are crying out for, companies can nurture their workforce as humans not machines.

The survey also found that 67% of young workers rated their mental health as a "very important" priority in their lives, higher than financial security (66%), relationships (66%), and work-life balance (60%). Gaga's "Be There Certificate" is a tool for how young people can support one another during difficult times, and can serve as a model for every workplace, family, and community.

Let's explore a meditation to radiate and sing kindness, inspired by Gaga:

Take a deep breath in and out, and as you exhale, let go of any stress or tension you may be holding onto.

Imagine yourself surrounded by a bright, warm light, a symbol of the kindness and compassion that Lady Gaga embodies.

As you inhale, imagine yourself filling up with this light, allowing it to permeate every part of your being, nourishing your mind, body and spirit.

As you exhale, imagine yourself spreading this light to others, radiating kindness and understanding to those around you.

Don't let your thoughts of concern, planning or judginess get in the way of this. Your mental health and wellness are vital to the entire planet because we are all connected, and it's crucial to take time for yourself to prioritize your well-being.

Repeat to yourself, "I am safe, I am guided and I am connected to all things. I am an expression of the Milky Way galaxy and I am here for a reason. I am creating a kinder planet earth!"

Now, begin to repeat the words "KINDER PLANET EARTH!" as beautifully as you can. Start to hum or sing these words to yourself with the feeling that you're singing to the center of the universe or to all the presidents of the globe.

Once you're ready to come to the end of this creative meditation, take one final deep breath in and out, knowing that you are capable of radiating kindness across the globe, simply by breathing and being in this vibration.

CYCLES OF LIFE

Why are we shooting @ stars

with guns made of stars?

If bullets and weapons are

Made from a metallic galaxy far

Away, why do we think we can shoot down Mars?

Just because we're angry in the bar,

Doesn't mean we can shoot down fear like RAWR!

But if the fight must be, let's spar...

With our higher selves, a war

That kills only bad choices, on par,

With everyone, none less, none better, on guard

To watch the mind from its thoughts crashing like cars.

To defend our Gods from hate, no matter how hard.

If such terror is stopped, then what's the prob?

If such freedom is free, then what's the charge?

It's ok if you're Homer but don't hate Marge

Just cause she makes babies, tends the home at-large

Helps us be the Lisa's in a world of Bart's.

Bigger question is: can food be killed if everything's a fart?

In the great spell of life, earth rearranged is just heart.

Garden's compost dying seeds to become plants, like art.

Who is the plot's enemy if all we do is act a different part?

Who am I really if I'm the gun, the bullet and

the reincarnated heart?

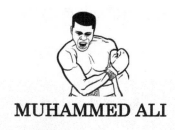

MUHAMMED ALI

"If my mind can conceive it, if my heart can believe it--then I can achieve it."

Throughout history, it's often ordinary people that catapult into influence because of their extraordinarily loving hearts. There's no better example of how ferocious and powerful a loving heart is than the iconic Muhammed Ali, born Cassius Clay. Cassius grew up in Louisville, Kentucky at a time when the south was segregated and he experienced discrimination throughout his childhood. When he was 12, his bike was stolen and he first felt the need to fight. He chased down the perpetrator and challenged him to a duel that would stand in archetypal memory for Cassius. Justice was the original motivation for a career that would change the modern world.

"I done wrestled with an alligator, I done tussled with a whale; handcuffed lightning, thrown thunder in jail; only last week, I murdered a rock, injured a stone, hospitalized a brick; I'm so mean I make medicine sick."

This was the trash-talking lexicon of pro boxing's greatest battle rapper, and Cassius was the original. He used his gift of gab and confident method of thinking to outwit and psych-out any opponent on or off the ring. This tactic, though seemingly commonplace today, was a riveting display of the power of the mind to overcome any opponent or obstacle.

But the Champ left as profound a legacy outside of the ring as he did inside. Aside from being the first rapper-boxer with poetic genius braggadocio, Muhammad Ali dedicated his life to service. From his hometown to villages around the world, he worked tirelessly for religious, ethnic and racial equality. Ali traveled to learn about the people of the earth, inspiring religious tolerance, supporting hundreds of millions of dollars of giving and even inspiring the Special Olympics, Make-A-Wish Foundation and endless organizations doing critical work for a better world.

"I've always wanted to be more than just a boxer," Ali said. "More than just the three-time heavyweight champion. I wanted to use my fame, and this face that everyone knows so well, to help uplift and inspire people around the world."

Inspired by Ali's legacy, here's a confidence-building activity (especially best before engaging in a challenging task) is to find a mirror and sit in front of it with a few deep breaths to start. Now, go ahead and recite one of his famous quotes, such as "I am the greatest" or "I am the king of the world," and repeat it to oneself.

Next, no matter how awkward, try increasing the volume of those same affirmative statements over and over until you are flexing muscles and jumping up & down in the air! Feeling yourself as successful in this moment, as Ali often did before a fight, can help embody the old statement: "Faith is the substance of things hoped for, the evidence of things not seen."

As you settle into a deep inner confidence, close your eyes and bring to mind the famous quote, "Float like a butterfly, sting like a bee!" during this mirror-meditation session. This quote emphasizes the importance of being light on your feet and quick in your movements, both physically and mentally. Focus on the sensation of floating and moving lightly, and imagine oneself being graceful and effective in how you interact with the world. Breathe into the feeling and let a smile radiate onto your face with clear confidence. Watch out world! You're ready to go out and spread this powerful energy!

JUST TO SHINE

At some point in time, we forgot that sunlight

Is the best disinfectant; that we are actually made

of light to shine.

We got lost, sick and tired, playing hide & seek with the blind.

Stuck inside of screen life, beaming shadows, scars and pride,

Complaining about the mirrors reflection online,

We thought fakes were real and reality was AI'd.

But what if we're too much hue, man, without being kind?

Stuck in patterns, our history repeats and it rhymes.

We used to be gardeners, sailors and builders of shrines

Now we're psychologists who hate the mind

Businessmen who hate the items line

Politicians who hate the people, why again?

We've become animals raised by threat or chide

clothes to cover all we are scared of - why hide!

We are all friends & enemies just changing sides.

Have we stolen everything in the name of money-time?

Outlawing women's bodies, choices and smiles?

We've turned Eve into a trafficked girl, streaming live

We've turned Eden into deserts, forests from

Amazonas to prime.

But who are we really when the funeral bells still chime?

Who are we if we still need a mother's love to thrive?

What can we do to let go of our pride?

What is the meaning of this precious life?

And where is the best place to breathe in quiet sunlight?

PARAMAHANSA YOGANANDA

"Be as simple as you can be; you will be astonished to see how uncomplicated and happy your life can become."

Born in 1893 in Gorakhpur, India to a devout and well-to-do Bengali family, Yogananda lost his mother at an early age and turned to God. He was praying and meditating from the early age of 4 and this devotional way of being never went away! In his youth, he sought out many of India's great sages and saints, hoping to find a teacher who would guide him on his spiritual quest. Fortunately, he met great teachers who initiated him into the path of Yoga, a way of life that became a blessing for the entire world.

As a student of the 5,000 year old practice of Yoga, the ancient practice of harmonizing the body with the spirit, Yogananda embodied the ancient science with a grace and capacity to reach the quickly changing modern industrial world. Through deep breathwork (pranayama), specific physical postures (asana) and meditation, Yoga is a daily practice of healing, strengthening and pacifying the mind. Yogananda mastered the thousands of techniques, practices and philosophies associated with this tradition and was sent by his teachers to help share the teachings of yoga to the Western world. He set out to prove an underlying unity or common wisdom between Eastern and Western religious or spiritual traditions. Would it be possible to achieve such shared inspiration given the vast divide of ancient Eastern mysticism vs the furious capitalistic materialism of the West?

Throughout the 20th century, as the rise of Western empire sought more and more external domination, teachers like Yogananda circled the globe with nothing more than love in their hearts and the tools needed for self-realization. He reached millions of people, met with presidents and started major yoga centers in cities across the US. These teachings have prepared millions in the western world for the rise (and fall) of materialism without bounds, simply by turning the focus on the heart, mind and body. Yogananda's "plain living and high thinking" principles attracted people from all walks of life and continues to inspire genuine awakening for seekers everywhere.

The ancient founder of Yoga, Patanjali, originally discovered Yoga as a precise and specified method to bring peace to body, mind and spirit. However, there are infinite Yogic practices to realize this noble goal without the harsh or strict regimes of the forest dwelling and metaphysical devotees of spiritual India. The famous "Sun Salutation" is a great place to start and can be modified for any body type or experience, from heavy athleticism to simple breathwork.

Traditionally, Sun Salutation is a series of postures that are performed in a specific sequence, usually 12 or more poses but please modify as your body dictates. The practice is typically done in the morning, facing the sun, and is said to help increase flexibility, strength, and balance, as well as improve mental focus and clarity. The specific postures and sequence of the practice may vary depending on the specific tradition or teacher, but generally includes a combination of standing and seated poses, as well as inversions and twists.

The traditional sun salutation sequence, Surya Namaskar in Sanskrit, usually consists of a breath-focused movement facing the eastern sunrise:

- Tadasana. Standing with your hands at your heart center, breathe in and reach up to the sky. With a long exhale, bow forward until your hands touch your feet.
- Urdhva Hastasana & Uttanasana. As you breathe in again, lift your head up in a flat back half lift with hands on thighs or shins. On the outbreath, drop your head again.
- Anjaneyasana. With the next in-breath, bring one of your legs back like a runner about to take off at a track meet. If you're able, you can rotate your back foot down to flat and then lift your arms up in prayer posture with the in-breath.
- Phalakasana & Chaturanga Dandasana. Drop your hands down on the outbreath and bring your body to a flat plank pose (like you're about to do a push-up).
- Urdhva Mukha Svanasana. On the in-breath, bring your chest to the floor and lift your head up.
- Adho Mukha Svanasana. Next, bring your butt up like a dog stretching until your body has reached an upside down V-shape with flat feet and flat hands, if possible.
- Anjaneyasana. You can bring your opposite foot forward now on the in-breath and then both feet come forward afterward to a forward fold.
- Uttanasana & Urdhva Hastasana. Lift your arms and head up again to come all the way over your head and back to prayer posture with the outbreath.
- Tadasana. Landing your hands on either side of your body and your spine erect, you've returned to the mountain from whence you came. Enjoy the vibrant pulsing of energy, peace and presence you've created for yourself.

It is also common practice to repeat the sequence multiple times, usually 2-3 sets. Consult with a qualified yoga teacher if you are new to the practice, as this flow can be supported with proper alignment in each pose to prevent injury.

PERSPECTIVE

This information age is mostly out of formation and context!

In this rage of echo-chambers and post-facts,

perspective is a verified source, go check,

On yourself and your intuitive knowledge - go back -

To experience the wisdom of soul maps,

The ones that lead to your heart and belly,

The math, the science, the art of the mind & body

That part of you that knows who to trust at the party.

Because the news is only as real as the reader,

And paintings are only as beautiful as the viewer,

Perspective can be a prison or a passport,

A prism or or a bad sport.

It can be the difference to make a difference!

Like healthy forgiveness vs disease in vengeance.

And though we can't control life's circumstances,

we can control how we respond to them, come dance!

Critical thinking and mythical giving prevents rote and rot.

Like having a thought vs identifying as the thought!

In a moment of information overload, consult breath.

Then, with a bit of space between life and death...

You can choose to live, give and resurrect!

CARMEN CARCELEN

"One heart, from my country, can help a thousand of yours."

Care for others is often based on the wisdom that it feels better to give than take. It also reminds you that everything you give away comes back to you, although it might not be in the manner you imagined. Those who adopt this perspective tend to be happier, fulfilled and more successful in life.

One night in 2017, Carmen (a successful housekeeper and essential worker in Ecuador) invited 11 beleaguered Venezuelan migrants into her home for a meal and a decent night's sleep. It was a simple act of generosity and kindness. But amazingly, word of Carmen's shelter spread back to Venezuela and she realized this could be a greater means by which she could help the immigrant crisis in her country. Within years, Carmen fed and sheltered over 10,000 migrants with the barely adequate resources that she had made over the years.

Her home in northern Ecuador has become a haven for thousands of people fleeing the most difficult conditions. The 48-year-old mother-of-eight has been welcoming Venezuelans without condition, providing relief to migrants and refugees on their long, and increasingly-dangerous journey. She is also known for giving people hugs when they need it and rubbing their aching feet.

Inspired by Carmen's story, here's a big-hearted call-to-kindness: if you have the means, consider taking a day this year to feed or house those in need! This can involve researching organizations or groups that work with houseless or low-income individuals and families, and finding ways to partner with them to provide assistance. Consider the following when weighing the pros or cons of offering such support to the greater community:

- How can I identify individuals or families who are in need of food or housing?
- How can I ensure that the food or housing I provide is safe, nutritious, and appropriate for the recipients' needs and for my own as well?
- How can I provide this assistance in a way that is respectful and empowering for the recipients, rather than paternalistic or demeaning?
- How can I sustain this effort without feeling depleted, and potentially expand it to reach more people in need?
- How can I involve and engage a community of benefactors to support this effort?
- How can I measure the impact and effectiveness of my actions and make necessary adjustments?

Answering these questions and considering the potential challenges and solutions can help to inform a plan for providing direct assistance to those in need of food and housing.

LOVE IN THE HEART

We all come from the cosmos and return to it.

Even extraterrestrials or weirdo billionaires.

Our name "human" comes from the word "humus": organic soil!

Soil consists of everything from worms to stardust,

from trace minerals to a microbial orchestra

playing a 4 billion year old song in silence.

We need to humble ourselves to our humus-level origins.

Now more than ever!

ReGround.

ReGenerate.

ReImagine.

ReMind.

ReCreate.

ReNaturalize!

This is a process of remembering.

The 150,000 + years humans have been on earth

have married us all

to the botanical flora or fauna of life.

It's only been the last several hundred years

that we have divorced this paradise we call earth.

Falling in love again is as easy

as remembering the love of life.

(And finding a good lawyer!)

DR JIM DOTY

Ever heard of the neurosurgeon who collaborates with the Dalai Lama and develops groundbreaking research about the scientific & medical benefits of human kindness and altruism? This unique combination of morally-driven leadership, science and medicine converge beyond the scope of professional binaries in the life of Dr Jim Doty. Jim might be a doctor, an academic and an inventor but he's primarily a passionate defender of human goodness.

Throughout his career, Dr. Jim Doty has dedicated himself to exploring the neural foundations of compassion and its potential to promote mental and physical well-being, as well as longevity. According to him, cultivating a compassionate mindset can lead to a more fulfilling and purposeful existence. He has supported health clinics around the world and programs for the disabled, as well as programs for teens and adolescents affected by AIDS/HIV. He has supported research programs at a number of universities and has helped establish transformational leadership frameworks at multiple universities.

Dr. Doty is also the bestselling author of "Into the Magic Shop: A Neurosurgeon's Quest to Discover the Mysteries of the Brain and the Secrets of the Heart", which has been translated into almost 40 languages and editions. His book was used by the K-Pop music sensation, BTS, as the basis for their third album, "Love Yourself: Tear" in which there is a song called, "Magic Shop".

But above all the acclaim and success', Dr Doty thinks it his biggest task to live as a kind-hearted person who laughs often and cares deeply for others. The microscope must first point into our own hearts and minds in order for it to work best on others!

One thing we can gain from Dr. Jim Doty's research on the neural bases of compassion is the importance of actively cultivating compassion in our daily lives. One way to do this is by taking on a kindness challenge, such as committing to performing one act of kindness per day. This could be as simple as holding the door open for someone, leaving a note of encouragement for a colleague, or making a donation to a charity. By making a conscious effort to care, we can not only improve our own well-being, but also make a positive impact on those around us.

Let's also try a simple kindness meditation inspired by Dr Jim:

1. Start by finding a quiet and calm place to sit. Close your eyes and take a deep breath in, hold for a moment at the apex, and then exhale slowly.
2. As you focus on your breath, imagine the neural pathways in your brain lighting up with feelings of compassion and kindness. With each inhale, imagine these pathways becoming stronger and more interconnected. As you exhale, imagine any feelings of stress or negativity being released from your mind and body.
3. Now, bring to mind a situation that you would like to send compassion and kindness to. It can be as intimate as a personal financial struggle or as vast as a national war in a nearby country. Like a superhero blasting heart beams through the atmosphere of the infinite, imagine sending the situation a deep sonar of vibrational support! Visualize the entire place or issue being enveloped by a

bright, loving and compassionate light. Repeat in your mind, "I see the entire scenario through the eyes of love and kindness. I see the entire situation resolved with peace, prosperity and grace. I see it being resolved now!"

4. As you continue to focus on this scenario being resolved, notice any feelings of warmth or compassion that may arise in your own heart. Allow these feelings to grow and expand, filling your entire body with a sense of loving-kindness.

5. When you're ready, take one more deep breath in and exhale, and slowly open your eyes.

Remember to carry this feeling of compassion and kindness with you throughout your day, and to be mindful of opportunities to act with compassion towards others as you adventure outward.

NO BEGINNING, NO END

... The oldest love story ever written

was a wordless ballet dance between

the mother earth and the father sun ...

they've been in love for years, billions,

With trillions of babies learning and unlearning

everyday how to co-exist, in motion.

A story that's being created at this very moment.

The mushrooms are the producers, directors.

The trees are the costume designers, protectors.

The microbes do casting and craft services.

The humans are the stage hands and superlatives.

The bugs are the orchestra, turning pages of lands.

The story has no beginning and never ends ...

TREVOR NOAH

"I realize that if I love myself and I have friends
that love me and family that loves me, I exist in a
constant state of love."

In our modern world built on the backs of the victims of racism
and others oppressed by unjust systems, apartheid in South
Africa was one of the worst and most regressive. For example,
one of the "laws" was that there couldn't be any interracial sex.
Police and authorities could even violate private property by
peering into homes to make sure no illegal relationships were
getting hot and steamy. As fate would have it, Trevor Noah was
born into this ridiculous society in 1984: a crime for even being
conceived! His dad was a white Swizz man, and his mother was
a black woman of the Xhosa tribe, so Trevor has been a rebel of
love from the moment he was born.

Tragically, Noah couldn't see his dad in public and was
painstakingly raised by a single mother. Much of his childhood
was spent alone, though not lonely, as his profound imagination
and love for rebellion gave him the companionship most kids
yearn for. He was an imaginative rascal, getting into trouble for
playing with knives, pyrotechnics and various pranks in the
township. Despite his family being poor, his mother taught him
languages from around the world and gave him a cultural
appreciation for all peoples. She managed to buy him books and
educate him on racism, classism and how to navigate his
complex identity.

His journey into racial and class solidarity wasn't just cultivated at home. Being poor, he yearned for the resources to buy his own things, so he began an enterprise in pirated CDs at school. He worked for a white student named Andrew, who he met after overhearing him complain about being ripped off by Black students. Noah offered to collect payment from them in exchange for a fee and also convinced his mother to buy him a computer for school work. Andrew taught Noah how to improve his computer and download music. When Andrew graduated, he gave Noah his CD burner, allowing him to start his own business. Noah was successful in the bootleg market by catering to diverse tastes and offering mixed CDs with fade in & out tracks. He became financially independent and used his success to help marginalized communities by recognizing the importance of resources and opportunities.

When apartheid finally ended, it made for new problems between tribal communities as to who would take power. The Zulus and Xhosas fought a bloody civil war that took many lives and left many struggling with how to heal. Since Noah was coming of age at this time, his strength was tested over and over. One day, when his family had to take the bus to church because their car was not working, the bus driver, who was Zulu, got into a disagreement with Noah's mother during the ride home. The driver told his mom he would teach her a lesson and sped up so she and her kids couldn't get off. The family had to pry the bus door open while it was speeding through the streets and jump out of the moving vehicle!

With a comedic knack for human psychology, Trevor's proficiency in race-class peacemaking helped transform his own tribulations into triumphs while helping others do the same. From the small businesses he ran at school playgrounds to clowning on societal ills as a comedian, Trevor broke free from the limitations of his upbringing and built a career aimed at collective liberation. As the host of The Daily Show, he utilized his platform to shed light on intersectionality and the bleeding lines between racism, classism and the destruction of the global environment. His unique ability to make audiences laugh while thinking critically has led to positive changes in society.

A race-class empathy exercise, inspired by Trevor's life:

1. Sit in a peaceful environment and close your eyes with deep breaths to ground your mind into the center of your heart space.
2. Remind yourself that empathy means trying to understand and share the feelings of others. We're going to practice empathy by imagining what it might be like to live in a different neighborhood or a different family from our own.
3. Imagine walking down a street in a neighborhood that is different from our own. We might imagine houses that are bigger or smaller, or yards that are neat or messy. We might imagine the people who live on the street, and how we might be different from the people we know.
4. After a few minutes, we can open our eyes and write one thing we imagined as a skit or short story.
5. Next, we can imagine walking into a house that is different from our own. We might imagine a house that is less or more tidy, or that has different types of furniture. We might imagine the people who live in the house, and how they might be different from the people we know.
6. After a few minutes, let's open our eyes again and write one thing we imagined in this scenario as a skit or short story.

7. Finally, let's think about how the people we imagined might feel, and how they themselves might feel if they lived in our neighborhood or house. Remember, empathy is an important skill to have, and that it can help us all to better understand and appreciate people who are different from ourselves.

~~~~~~

KINDNESS TO PLANET

~~~~~~

CIRCLE OF

KINDNESS

FAITH PRESENCE HUMILITY
CREATIVITY LISTENING COMPASSION FORGIVENESS SERVICE
WONDER BREATH GRATITUDE JOY
REST SELF-CARE
VULNERABILITY HUMOR PATIENCE
PRESEVERANCE

INNER=SELF MIDDLE=OTHERS OUTER=PLANET

KINDNESS TO PLANET

Imagine you're outside gardening in order to grow healthy food for your family and rebuild soil organic-matter at a time when science (and common sense) says these are crucial services for our bodies and planet. Now imagine you're also receiving Vitamin D from the sun, connecting with immune-system building microbes and cultivating bacteria that improves life satisfaction. Your digging in the dirt lifts your spirit by stirring and inhaling microbes that stimulate your serotonin production, which makes you feel relaxed and happier. All because of the science of being kind to the earth!

According to the esteemed Dr. David R. Hamilton, acts of kindness such as being kind to the earth through gardening, create emotional warmth, which releases hormones known as serotonin and oxytocin. Oxytocin causes the release of a chemical called nitric oxide, which dilates the blood vessels, supports brain functioning and strengthens the nervous system. Serotonin is a chemical that carries messages between nerve cells in the brain and throughout your body. Serotonin plays a key role in such body functions as mood, sleep, digestion, nausea, wound healing, bone health, blood clotting and sexual desire. What's more, cultivating good soil releases both serotonin and oxytocin; a natural antidepressant!

Let's go even further. A study recently examined the bacteria, "Mycobacterium Vaccae", in soil. It has indeed been found to mirror the effect on neurons that drugs like Prozac provide! Studies were conducted on cancer patients and they reported a better quality of life with less stress. These antidepressant microbes in soil may be as easy to use as playing in the dirt with a child or building organic matter in your soil through composting and mulching.

Being kind to the earth through gardening, regenerative farming, or environmental conservation not only protects and preserves the natural environment and its resources, but it also has the power to make you happier and healthier. So why not try incorporating organic gardening, composting, and mulching in your weekly routine and see the positive effects it brings to both the earth and your well-being?

CELIA XAKRIABA'

'We are only 5% of the world's population [but] 80% of biodiversity is protected by indigenous peoples. It is a humanitarian commitment, because only those who know how to be animals, who know how to be seeds, earth and trees, know how to be human."

While many teens were eating fries and watching TV, a 13 year old Célia Xakriabá courageously entered the National Congress of Brazil to make a statement on behalf of her people, the Xakriabá tribe of the Amazon. 19 years later, her dream became a reality as she became the first indigenous woman in the state of Minas Gerais to be elected federal deputy. This victory was the result of a collective effort by the indigenous movement, called the "Bancada do Cocar," to expand the representation of native peoples in politics and stop the horrific attacks on the natural world. Steeped in generational wisdom, Célia's mission prioritized preserving cultural heritage, recognizing ancestral wisdom in education, and promoting socio-environmental justice.

To give some context as to why Celia's struggle grew to global prominence, let's acknowledge some facts: in Brazil, deforestation is an emergency issue that contributes to carbon emissions and reduces biodiversity worldwide. In 2020 alone, under Bolsonaro's regime, 11,088 km² of forest were deforested, which is more than three times the legal limit. Deforestation has affected over 20% of the Amazon, with 40% of the forest under human pressure. Indigenous peoples are the main stewards of a biodiverse and healthy forest, having built ancient relationships of symbiosis unbroken for thousands of years. They are at the forefront of the fight to protect their territories and nature, despite the State's control and surveillance. And despite the obvious need for respect, they face opposition from those wanting to burn the land for animal agriculture or mineral extraction industries.

In a poetic letter written for Earth Day 2020, entitled "We Are The Earth", Celia wrote with fellow indigenous leader Sônia Guajajara the following acuity: *"We are the Earth. We arise from the Earth and we return to it. The Earth is within us... Who are we? We are the original peoples. We sprout from the ashes of burnt trunks. Even when pruned, we know how to regrow. For five hundred years we have resisted the commodification of life, and those who want to tear our roots from our territory, to fracture our world, our common land. We have resisted all the fences that have deprived us of our territories. We have resisted the massacres, the invisibility to which we have been subjected, the attempts to exterminate our existence and annihilate our culture. Today the Earth once again calls our name. We are interpreters of its clamour."*

Since that fateful day as a teenager, Célia has long worked as an advisor to lawmakers, helping create policies for environmental protection and education. Disappointed from year after year of elected officials who did not prioritize the people's interests, she decided to run for office herself. In 2022, she made history as the first indigenous woman from her tribe to be elected. With support from indigenous territories and quilombola communities, she was third in the popular vote in Belo Horizonte. In 2023, she brings the hopes and needs of her people to Brasília, determined to make a difference in the fight against corrupt government or business.

The main challenge she wants to overcome is the "racism of absence," the idea that indigenous people have no place in institutional politics. She wants to change this and be a voice for her people. "Our representation does not mean that the problems will be solved. On the contrary: we will have a voice and a possibility of decision with the pen, but mobilization is what sustains us," she says.

In her work as a federal deputy, Célia Xakriabá is inspired by the wisdom of her indigenous tribe, the Xakriabá, as well as other indigenous Amazonian communities. One important principle she incorporates into her practice is the idea of ayni, or reciprocity and mutual support. Ayni is the practice of giving and receiving in a way that creates balance and fosters community.

For Célia, this means working to build relationships of trust and support with the other parliamentarians and members of the indigenous movement, and being available to listen to and learn from their perspectives. It also means being a strong advocate for the rights and needs of her community and other indigenous peoples, and working tirelessly to advance their causes.

This practice of kindness and reciprocity is essential to the success of the Bancada do Cocar, the front that Célia is a part of and which seeks to expand the representation of indigenous peoples in institutional politics. By building strong relationships of trust and support, they are better able to work together to achieve their shared goals and overcome obstacles.

The takeaway for us is that the practice of ayni can serve as a powerful model for fostering collaboration and cooperation within communities and organizations. By being open to giving and receiving, and by being supportive and available to each other, groups can work together more effectively and achieve their goals.

Here is a meditation inspired by Celia, focusing on the interconnectedness of the Amazon rainforest and our planet's well-being:

1. Find a quiet, comfortable place to sit and close your eyes. Take a deep breath in and exhale slowly.
2. Visualize yourself standing in the midst of the Amazon rainforest. Imagine the lush, green canopy above you, the sounds of the forest around you, and the rich, earthy scent of the forest floor.
3. As you look around, imagine the countless trees and plants that make up the rainforest, all working together to create a delicate balance. See the way the trees take in carbon dioxide and release oxygen, providing us with the vital air we need to breathe.
4. Think about how the Amazon rainforest acts as the earth's lungs, producing 20% of the world's oxygen and helping regulate the global climate.
5. Take another deep breath and feel the oxygen from the rainforest entering your body. Imagine the oxygen nourishing your cells and giving you energy.
6. Now imagine the effects of deforestation and the destruction of the rainforest or the peoples who steward its biodiversity. See how this would disrupt the delicate balance and harm our planet's health.

7. Take a moment to acknowledge the interdependence of all life on this planet and the importance of protecting the Amazon rainforest.

8. Exhale slowly and when you're ready, open your eyes. Take a moment to integrate this experience into your daily life, remembering the impact our actions have on the health of the planet and committing to making choices that support the well-being of the rainforest and all life on earth.

I AM BECAUSE YOU ARE

There's an ancient Mayan word: InLakesh.

A few definitions of what it means are: I am because you are!

Or we are individual drops of rain

but falling into a common ocean

To me it sums up the best of my reflections about

being a parent

I feel as though my life's purpose

is for your existence and well being, yes!

If you get hurt, I get hurt.

If you're in pain, I am in pain.

By the same token, when you smile I smile.

If you feel healthy, I feel healthy.

It's a magic potion of mutuality,

That connects us forever and forever

Yea yea yea yea

We are one family

Yea yea yea yea

We are one family

Yea yea yea yea

We are one family

Ubuntu,

Henosis,

Tikun Olam,

148

Hongi Greeting,

Namaste

Science of togetherness

It's in all ancient original ways on earth

I guess it's just how you look at it

One person's trash is another person's treasure

So why not get rich and heal the planet!

Heal the planet, heal ourselves.

I am because you are.

Heal the planet, heal ourselves.

I am because you are …

YVON CHOUINARD

"You learn that how you got there was what's important. Not what you accomplished."

As a young adventurer searching for a falcon's nests, Yvon discovered rock climbing almost by happy accident. To save money, and make adaptations for the wild way he was climbing, he decided to make his own climbing tools, teaching himself blacksmithing. He eventually started a business. Between time spent surfing and climbing, he sold his creations out of the back of his car to support himself.

These new creations for ecological exploration - alongside his book *Climbing Ice* (1978) - started the modern sport of ice climbing. It took innovation after innovation with many different tools to realize that even the most successful "bestseller" isn't worth wrecking the environment it's being used for. Clean climbing was born!

Chouinard is best known for founding the clothing and gear company Patagonia. In 1970 on a trip to Scotland, he purchased some rugby shirts and sold them with great success. From this seed, the Patagonia company developed a wide selection of rugged technical clothing that attempted to be as ecologically-clean as possible. Recognizing that the financial success of the company provided the opportunity to also achieve personal goals, Chouinard committed the company to being an outstanding place to work, and to be an important resource for global environmental activism.

Patagonia opened an on-site cafeteria offering "healthy, mostly vegetarian food," and started providing on-site child care. Chouinard committed the company to "tithing" for environmental activism, committing one percent of sales or ten percent of profits, whichever is the greater. The commitment included paying employees working on local environmental projects so they could commit their efforts full-time.

In 1996, Chouinard committed the company to using all organic cotton. In 2002, Yvon Chouinard founded 1% for the Planet and Patagonia became the first business to commit 1% of annual sales to the environment. Now it's the first company to have ever made the earth its only shareholder!

Patagonia supports advocacy documentary filmmaking, including stories like *DamNation*, changing attitudes in America towards its dams. Chouinard was the executive producer of the film, and he was also featured in the film commenting about dams. The courageous kindness of that explorative boy who loved nature has led to tremendous changes in the corporate sector as well as public advocacy.

Here's a nature adventure challenge inspired by Yvon:

1. Pick a local trail or park that you've never been to before.
2. Plan a one-day hiking or camping trip to this location.
3. Before you go, research the trail or park and learn about the natural history, the flora/fauna and the original peoples of those lands.
4. Bring adequate food/water/safety supplies, along with a journal and sketchbook to document your adventure. If you can, please challenge yourself to leave your phone and camera behind!
5. During the hike or camping trip, take the time to really observe and appreciate your natural surroundings. Notice the different textures and colors of the plants, the

shapes and movements of the animals, and the sounds of the wilderness.

6. Take a moment to reflect on how much joy nature brings to the world and why that's so important to protecting it.
7. When you return home, share your experience with friends, colleagues and family, and encourage them to get out and explore nature too!

This challenge is not only a great way to connect with nature and appreciate the beauty of the outdoors, but also to understand the importance of caring for it by way of building a relationship with it.

QUESTION EVERYTHING

"We question all of our beliefs except those that we believe and those we never think to question." What is a belief but a calcified thought form, strengthened by years of subconsciousness patterning or environmental influences? And what is a question but a willingness to learn; to decalcify our beliefs and patterns for a brave jump beyond the known reality. Have you ever realized that you were wrong about something without feeling shame? Have you ever realized that you were right about something without feeling vanity? What beliefs or certainties do you have now that could use a shaking up or elevation?

Someone once asked a blind person to describe the color red and was surprised to hear that red is a feeling and an internal quality beyond the visible. Someone once asked a deaf person what music sounds like? They responded by putting their hands to their heart and dancing peacefully with a smile. Someone once asked a child what adulthood is like and they responded by counting some dollars in an imaginary wallet and then yelling at a wall before falling over laughing. Someone once asked a person on their deathbed what the afterlife is all about and they responded by sharing this:

"To me, the so-called after-life is this life, except it's expressed in the invisible form of one universal energy flow lacking any duality or opposition. It's not a place, it's a grace. It's not a Yes or a No, it's a Yo. It's not a business that did well or a government with all the power, it's a luminous circle around a fireplace where all is celebrated. It's not an answer or a question, it's a wordless dream that lives in all of us."

LENG OUCH

"Even though I know my life is at risk, I still try to save the forest"

A young boy named Leng was deeply connected to the natural world. Growing up in the forests of Cambodia, he spent his childhood exploring the diverse ecological playground that was his universe. Nature was his sanctuary, his teacher, and his best friend. This was home.

However, as Leng grew older, he began to witness firsthand the destruction of these precious forests at the hands of illegal logging and commercial exploitation. Determined to make a difference, Leng decided to use his knowledge of the forest and his passion for conservation to fight back against these destructive practices.

With the help of new technologies like cameras, GPS trackers, and drones, Leng set out to document and expose the illegal logging activities that were devastating his beloved forest. He also built a network of informants within the logging industry, gaining valuable insight into the corruption and greed that drove these destructive practices.

Despite the many dangers that environmental activists face in Cambodia, Leng was fearless in his commitment to protecting his ancestral homeland. He bravely went undercover to document illegal logging activities, using his footage to raise awareness and call for solidarity from the global community.

Thanks to Leng's tireless efforts, many large land concessions were canceled, and many rural communities were able to protect their land and livelihoods.

As Leng grew older, he realized that the forest had always been a part of him. The saying "You can take the child out of the forest but you can't take the forest out of the child" is almost made for Leng. He will always be fiercely dedicated to protecting the natural world that has given him so much. His efforts not only helped to preserve the forest but also served as an inspiration for others to take up the cause for conservation and preservation of nature.

Let's create a conservation meditation, inspired by Leng! To begin, find a quiet and comfortable place to sit. Close your eyes and take a deep breath in, hold for a moment, and then exhale slowly.

Imagine yourself standing in the midst of a lush forest, just like the one where Leng spent his childhood. See the tall trees reaching up to the sky, the dense underbrush, and the vibrant wildlife that calls this place home.

Take in the beauty of this natural world. Focus on the feeling of connection and gratitude that you have for this place. Imagine yourself walking through the forest, breathing in all of the sights, sounds, and smells.

As you walk, picture the devastation caused by illegal logging, pollution, and other human activities that threaten the survival of these ecosystems.

Take a deep breath in, and as you exhale, imagine yourself becoming Leng, standing up for your mind's forest and working tirelessly to protect it. Feel the determination and courage that he had, and let it fill you up.

As you continue to walk through your imaginal forest, visualize yourself taking actions to protect this place. Caring for the herbs, insects or trees, cleaning up litter and using your voice and your resources to educate or create more protected places.

When you're ready, take one more deep breath in and exhale, and slowly open your eyes.

GIVING IS RECEIVING

We spaceship through the stars beaming

With pride, as if money buys us meaning

But what if giving was our receiving?

What if acquiring was actually just feeling

All needs met, the race to be alive is no competing

Living in the energy of already having

We're bees, we die when we're grasping or stinging

We live best when we're offering not needing

The irony is it's all inside-out like a heart bleeding

To love, to be kind, to forgive everything

Why seek answers outside ourselves screaming

@ a phone when our thoughts are what needs cleaning?

Like IPO'ing Amazon wheeling & dealing

yet almost lost the real thing believing

In fake paper more than tree leafs greening

Valuing computers more than fresh apples eating

Fast fooding while our bellies are slowing & screaming

Inflamed by the flames of mal-digesting

Who cares how many brands are winning

Versus how many indigenous bands are cultivating

Habitat and wisdom for the next 7 generations singing!

It's the difference between thinking

Of a bank account vs a river bank account · chi ching!

Our path through the stars needs a new bottom-lining.

JADAV PAYENG

"Only by growing plants will the earth survive ... I'll plant till my last breath!"

A teenager named Jadav Payeng was walking along a dried-up river and found hundreds of snakes dead in a kind of mass suicide. How odd, he thought! He realized that it was heat and flooding that had killed these snakes in an area that had become desertified. Only 19 - but wise beyond his years in the wisdom of the land - this young man resolved to regreen the area with bamboo. He sourced water from extended irrigation and cared for the plants like they were his children. When he saw that it was working, he realized that he might as well keep going, forever! All in all, he planted a tree everyday for 40 years. What has emerged out of an old desert is now a man-made forest bigger than Central Park!

This teenager's little forest, which came to be known as Molai forest, now provides habitat for everything from rabbit to deer, Bengal tigers to rhinoceros, monkeys and rare birds! Herds of elephants regularly visit the forest every year and live there for 6-7 months of the year! There are several thousand rare and common trees, from arjun (Terminalia arjuna) to ejar (Lagerstroemia speciosa), goldmohur (Delonix regia) to koroi Albizia procera), moj (Archidendron bigeminum) to himolu (Bombax ceiba). The microbial life of the soils are almost unmatched in terms of natural biodiversity, providing invisible yet profound benefits to the global climate and biodiversity tracker.

For a long while, Jadav's forest was quietly cultivated with nothing more than the villagers enjoying its benefits. One day, the forest department passed through in search of 115 rogue elephants and the officials were beyond shocked to find a dense and exotic forest having transformed the health and economy of the bioregion. For this reason, the forest is now a model for the nation and will commence to franchise onto other sandbar's or riparian passageways in need of repair or restoration.

That boy-wonder, now deemed a national treasure across India, vows to plant trees until his last breath! "Nature is God. It gives me inspiration. It gives me power. As long as it survives, I survive."

Are you ready to take on the Jadav Payeng Tree Planting Challenge? Here's how you can participate:

1. Choose a location in your community where you would like to plant trees. This could be a park, a school, or even your own backyard.
2. Research the best tree species for the location and climate in your area. Consider factors such as water needs, sunlight requirements, and the type of soil.
3. Purchase or acquire the tree seedlings and any necessary tools for planting them.
4. Set a goal for yourself, whether it's planting one tree a week for a year or a certain number of trees in a specific period of time.
5. Get to work! Plant your tree(s) and care for them as they grow.
6. Share your progress with others. Take pictures of your trees and post them on social media, using the hashtag

#JadavPayengTreePlantingChallenge. Encourage your friends and family to join in and plant trees of their own.

7. Reflect on the impact of your actions. As you watch your trees grow, feel the positive impact they will have on the environment, the community, and future generations.

HOME IS WHERE THE HEARTH IS

How would you rate your experience on earth so far?

Would you count the best days or feel dazed by the count?

Have you found a secret spot in nature ⁃

where you can finally unplug your phone

and plug in to the scent of your previous breath?

Have you befriended any plants or trees in your neighborhood?

What is your favorite medicinal herb?

What is your favorite culinary herb?

What's your favorite rock, stone or crystal?

In times of crisis, do you turn to the earth or to the machines?

They say home is where the heart is.

Home is also the hearth.

Earth is our hearth.

Earth is our home in the stars.

We hope you're feeling the miracle of wherever you are.

AFROZ SHAZ

"When we hold hands and attempt a difficult task - we accomplish it."

They say that "faith can move mountains". But can it clean up all the mess we've created on earth? According to Afroz Shaz, the answer is yes. That's because young people will do the thing everyone says is impossible just as the naysayers finish printing their critique! Simply because it must be done!

Afroz is one of those champions of the impossible. A true hero of kindness to the planet. He started picking up trash from a local Mumbai beach back in 2015, with more and more people joining him until the project snowballed into hundreds of volunteers managing to pick up 5.3 million kilograms of trash! This was the world's largest beach clean-up project and has grown into a movement inspiring volunteers worldwide to clean up their surrounding bioregions.

Versova Beach in Mumbai was polluted mainly because of the direction of the wind. Since the territory itself was not a popular tourist attraction, there was no action taken to take care of the beach. Now, with the help of 1,000 volunteers, the beach is open for the public to enjoy. As a result, the United Nations named Shah as a Champion of the Earth for this courageous random act of kindness. Inspired by Shah's effort to clean beaches in Mumbai, the UNEP launched the Clean Seas campaign globally because there are over 8 billion tons of plastic thrown into our ocean every year.

If you wish to reduce your plastic waste try avoiding single-use cutlery, take away coffee cups, use your own grocery bag instead of plastic one, and buy as many plastic-free products as you can. REFUSE. REDUCE. REUSE. RECYCLE.

Even more so, demand governments and corporations clean up their supply chains and innovate their packaging or products materials to reflect a kinder footprint on the planet. Individual actions are great but whole system actions are crucial to facing the scale of the plastic pollution emergency worldwide.

NURTURE OUR NATURE

People are made from equal parts Nature & Nurture,
but we've built systems that ignore both.
A simple walk in the woods
with friends reminds us
Nature and Nurture are waiting for us everywhere...
if we can only slow to the speed of life
and feel their healing presence.

The ancient practice of forest bathing
is a slowing down way
to explore local parks or wildlands:
Originating as a mindfulness practice
in Japan, it's called "shinrin-yoku"...
A simple practice that helps
heighten senses to experience nature
At the speed of the breath.

HANSJÖRG WYSS

"I am very grateful for the opportunities I've had and feel I have a duty to repay my good fortune through philanthropic endeavors that expand the reach of human possibility and compassion."

Where does generosity and goodwill to humanity and the planet come from? Some might say it's learned. Others might argue it's an innate gift that you're born with. Perhaps it's both. This old "Nature vs Nurture" debate is alive and well in the iconic life story of Hansjorg Wyss. According to *Forbes*, Wyss is "among the most philanthropic people in the world".

Between 2004 and 2008 alone, *Businessweek* estimated that Wyss personally donated nearly US$277 million. In 2013, he signed The Giving Pledge, agreeing to give away the majority of his fortune. The assets of his charitable foundations equal nearly $2 billion. He has made major donations to environmental, cultural and scientific causes, as well as progressive organizations. In 2019, Wyss promised to donate 20 million swiss francs to the Bern Art Museum. He made it a condition that the Hodlerstrasse, on which the museum is located, be free of cars. As of 2015, Wyss and the Wyss Foundation had donated more than $350 million to environmental protection, including conservation of national forests and other public lands in the Western United States.

True to the adage that "we can't save what we don't love", Wyss has said that he became passionate about land preservation after visiting the U.S. in 1958 as a student land-surveyor with the Colorado Highway Department. In 1998, he created the Wyss Foundation. The vision for the foundation was to sponsor informal partnerships between non-governmental organizations and the United States government, in order to place large swathes of land under permanent protection. The organization sponsors the Wyss Scholars Program for graduate-level education in conservation.

The landscape protection strategies of the foundation have included assisting the purchase of mineral leases from oil and gas companies to river restorations, ocean conservation in Peru and Canada, anti-poaching efforts in Africa, and environmental journalism across the globe.

In 2018, Wyss donated $1 billion to the Wyss Campaign for Nature, aiming to conserve 30% of the world's land and oceans by 2030. $1 billion dollars to protect our earth! In an article titled "We Have to Save the Planet. So I'm Donating $1 Billion", Mr. Wyss stated he is willing to donate this amount of money with the goal of protecting 30 percent of the planet's surface by 2030. May other billionaires and wealthy organizations adopt similar values and use their massive financial influence to bring more kindness to the planet.

Inspired by Hansjörg's visionary work, we would like you to help us put out a call for billionaires (and those of influence) to flex their moral muscles by addressing economic inequality, and associated crises:

We write to you today with a sense of urgency for an economic reform that could transform our world and bring about a free and just future for all: Universal Basic Income (UBI)!

First, let's introduce the concept of UBI. UBI is essentially conscious capitalism, where income doesn't start at 0. As was

166

recognized by the framers of the American Declaration of Independence, every person, by virtue of their being a living, breathing, sentient being, is granted the inalienable right to life, liberty, and the pursuit of happiness. An income that covers every person's basic needs, so that they automatically start out on the third level of Maslow's hierarchy of needs, not having to worry about how to afford the food and shelter they need to survive, is what is necessary to actually give them the security to freely pursue their happiness. The funding source, amount, and exact disbursement details of a UBI can vary, but a key component of the idea is that it be truly universal (i.e., unconditional), so that it is truly just and provides a financial floor for everyone in society to stand on.

One possible implementation of a UBI could be a tax credit strategy that provides a basic income to all individuals regardless of their employment status. Alternatively, it could come in the form of regular disbursements to individual bank accounts. Regardless, the ultimate goal is to eliminate poverty, thereby solving intersectional socio-environmental crises and increasing financial stability for our nations and world.

The idea of UBI has been around for centuries. Thomas Paine, in his 1797 book *Agrarian Justice*, argued that every citizen of the fledgling United States should be taken care of, but it gained significant attention in the 20th century as a solution to address economic inequality and unemployment.

Today, we are facing a global economic crisis that has only exacerbated existing inequalities. The COVID-19 pandemic has resulted in millions of job losses and economic instability for many families. In addition, our cultural and political strategies are failing to address the systemic issues of poverty, inequality and the environmental context that furthers these crises. We need a new approach that focuses on creating economic security for all, and UBI is the answer.

A UBI or Strategic UBI could be initially targeted towards specific demographics such as mothers, farmers and cultural stewards who have been disproportionately impacted by the economic downturn but are critical to the safety, health and innovation of our species. This would not only provide financial stability to these groups, but also create a ripple effect of economic growth as they are able to invest in their businesses and communities.

Billionaires, you have the power and resources to lead the charge towards a more equitable future. You have the ability to create change on a global scale and make a positive impact on millions of lives. By advocating for and implementing a UBI, you have the opportunity to be champions for so many important and critical solutions worldwide:

Here is a bullet list of some of the solutions we can address with UBI:

- Addressing the gender pay gap and providing financial support for mothers, especially single mothers, who face unique challenges in the workforce.
- Supporting artists and creatives who are often undervalued and underpaid, despite their contributions to society.
- Empowering farmers to invest in sustainable agriculture and support local food systems, which can lead to a healthier population, stronger communities and a restored biosphere.

- Reducing crime rates by addressing the root causes of poverty and providing financial stability to those who may turn to illegal activities out of desperation.
- Stimulating the economy by giving people the financial means to invest in local businesses and contribute to their communities.
- Providing a safety net for those who may not be able to work due to disability or illness, and ensuring that everyone has access to basic necessities like food and housing.

By implementing a strategic UBI, we can create a more just, compassionate and equitable society, where everyone has the opportunity to thrive and reach their full potential.

THE U.BEE.I

Once upon a lime tree, in a bustling beehive, all the bees worked tirelessly day and night to gather nectar and pollen to bring back to the hive. They worked hard, but they were never quite sure if they would have enough to survive the winter ahead.

One day, the Queen Bee proposed a new idea to the hive: "universal beesic income!" Under this new system, every bee would receive a certain amount of honey each month, regardless of their job or status in the hive.

At first, the bees were skeptical. They worried that if they didn't have to work as hard, the hive wouldn't have enough honey to survive. But the Queen Bee assured them that the hive would still thrive, and that the extra honey would allow them to focus on other important tasks, like building stronger combs, perfecting their dance communications and caring for the young bees.

So, the hive implemented universal beesic income and to everyone's surprise, thrived like never before! The bees were able to take time to explore new flowers and find new sources of nectar. They were able to focus on building stronger combs and caring for the young bees. They even had enough honey to share with other hives in need.

The hive became a shining example to all the other hives in the area, and soon, many of them adopted universal basic income as well. The bees realized that when they didn't have to worry about where their next meal would come from, they could focus on the things that truly mattered: building a strong community and taking care of each other. So the beehive prospered and all the bees lived happily ever after.

NEMONTE NENQUIMO

"I will confront what may come, without fear. Everything I do
is for life itself. And for my daughter."

Like ancestral whisperings through the songs of the forest itself,
Nenquimo has expressed a love for her land going back
generations. Her community, the Huaorani people, sometimes
called 'Waorani' or 'Wadoni,' are a traditionally semi-nomadic
hunter-forager-horticulturist indigenous group located in the
Ecuadorian Amazon. The Huaorani have traditionally
egalitarian relationships rather than hierarchical ones.
Individuals work together for the survival of the community as
a whole. Even children are fairly self-sufficient and aren't
considered to be inferior to adults. Men and women have slightly
different roles but have an equal role in decision making in
families. While some of the younger generations now keep track
of their age, it was not common to keep track of age in the past,
so life expectancy is unknown.

When Nemonte's Waorani tribes were first colonized in 1958 by
Christian missionaries and rubber or petrochemical companies,
many structural and ecological crises emerged. In the 1960s, the
Ecuadorian government, driven by its cravings for oil, started
building roads into untouched habitat and destroying ancestral
lands. The government also arbitrarily split Waorani lands to
auction for oil extraction. Most of the Ecuadorian Amazon has
been affected by this, with six of the blocks auctioned to oil
companies belonging to the Waorani. One of these blocks is
Nemompare, Nenquimo's birthplace. As a result, the Waorani

people have been forced to move further into the forest in a fight to remain independent from the outside world.

Sadly, this corrupt partnership between governments and petrochemical industries is a worldwide problem and at odds with the world's indigenous communities. What's more, the indigenous peoples of the world hold the key to biodiversity. Scientists have studied where the most intact ecosystems are and it always comes back to indigenous-led bioregions.

Nemonte says that her people felt the effects of climate change long before it became a global crisis. Impressively, she's found ways to use the law to fight governmental and corporate corruption. Her most famous lawsuit is the one filed against her own government. In 2019, the Waorani people successfully stopped oil drilling in the Ecuadorian rainforest – protecting 500,000 acres of the Amazon from exploitation, safeguarding lives and livelihoods, and establishing a legal precedent for regional indigenous rights. Thanks to fierce frontline leaders like Nemonte, we have a kinder, more just and more liveable planet for all to thrive.

An acknowledgement takeaway, inspired by Nemonte: There are several ways that individuals and organizations can support indigenous conservation efforts worldwide. Some examples include:

1. Supporting and promoting indigenous-led conservation initiatives. Many indigenous communities have a deep understanding and connection to the natural environments they live in, and have developed their own conservation practices. Supporting and promoting these initiatives can help ensure that they are successful in protecting the land and biodiversity.

2. Advocating for indigenous rights! Indigenous people are often marginalized and their rights are not always respected, which can make it difficult for them to protect their lands and resources. Advocating for the rights of indigenous people, such as the right to free, prior, and informed consent, can help ensure that they have a say in decisions that affect their lands and resources.
3. Supporting indigenous-led sustainable development. Many indigenous communities rely on their natural resources for their livelihoods. Supporting sustainable development initiatives that are led by indigenous communities can help ensure that these resources are used in a way that is both economically beneficial and environmentally sustainable.
4. Educating oneself about the history and culture of indigenous people. Indigenous people have often been misrepresented in mainstream media and history, and educating oneself about their history and culture can help build a deeper understanding and appreciation of their conservation efforts.
5. Supporting organizations working for Indigenous conservation. There are many organizations working towards conservation of Indigenous people and their land, you can support them by volunteering, donating, or spreading awareness about their work.

It is important to note that each indigenous community is unique and have their own ways of protecting their land and resources, it's important to support them in the way they deem appropriate.

PARENTING PLANETING

Parent
Am I your parent or your child?

Child
Um, dad you're being weird again...

Parent
Weird just means fated, or destined, to be ...

Child
I don't get it. Are you destined to be weird?

Parent
Well, after sacrificing my sleep for years and living in service to
you entirely, I think it must be so.

Child
Are you saying I'm worth it?

Parent
Beyond ... the best and hardest thing I've ever had ... you
literally grew me another heart!

Child
From weird to insane to comical to sappy to weird... that's my
lovely dad!

Parent
I can't help it! I just love you to the moon and back.

Child

I love you too … and … why can't we demand greener schools across the world? The planet is burning while we have the solutions to change the destructive system and restore balance for our biosphere … don't we all have a right to exist?!

Parent

Um … you're just proving my point - yet again - that you're the parent and I'm the child. Let's go!

XIAOYUAN REN

"We aim to help people understand the big environmental challenges we face, but also that solutions are within the reach of each of us."

Education is the key to success for many young girls around the world. A young girl named Ren was born and raised in Beijing, China, where her parents were both the first in their family to attend college. As a high school student, she became interested in environmental issues and joined a local chapter of Roots & Shoots, the international youth organization founded by Jane Goodall. What's more, her grandparents lived outside the city in a rural area, and their fights with polluted water were an influence on her future field of study. There are millions of people in China who do not have access to clean drinking water; pollution caused by industrial and agricultural chemical runoff is a significant problem in rural districts.

Ren used her passion for water and her hard work ethic in school to receive a Bachelor of Arts degree in physics from Vassar College and masters degrees in both Environmental Engineering and Technology Policy from Massachusetts Institute of Technology. For her graduate work, Ren studied rural water monitoring systems in India. This exploration developed into the ongoing MIT/India "Data for Improved Governance" project.

Ren first wrote a business plan for the company that would become MyH2O in 2014 during her postgraduate studies at MIT, with mentorship from engineer John H. Lienard V. She was inspired by the robust network of water quality and sanitation databases that she observed in India while completing her masters degrees. She launched the platform in 2015 with the goal of using similar data collection systems to combat a crisis of poor water quality in rural China.

Ren founded MyH2O on the crucial understanding that if environmental pollution is to be remediated, it must first be made visible. The MyH2O platform collects data on rural water quality and sanitation through a network of youth volunteers. The data collected is shared with policy makers and then used for the provision of clean water resources to rural communities. Data is made available to volunteers and residents via a dedicated mobile app, which also provides resources and guidance about purifying contaminated water. The MyH2O network covers 1,000 villages located across 26 provinces; the MyH20 app charts groundwater quality so that people can find clean sources of drinking water.

A meditation on water, inspired by Xiaoyuan:

1. Begin by pouring a glass of water into a sacred bowl or special glass that is special to you. Put the water on an altar or in front of you for meditation and find a comfortable seated position.
2. Close your eyes and take a few deep breaths in and out, and allow yourself to relax.
3. Imagine a beautiful, sparkling stream flowing from the water in front of you into a lush forest stream. See the water sparkling in the sunlight, and feel the coolness of the water as it flows over your skin.
4. Imagine that this stream is a symbol of the clean water that is available to everyone on earth. See people of all

ages, cultures, and backgrounds coming to the stream to drink, bathe, and play. See all the waters of the world being cleaned by way of this stream.

5. Visualize a world in which clean water is accessible to all, and all people have the opportunity to live healthy, fulfilling lives. See communities thriving, and feel the sense of peace and well-being that comes from having this basic need met.

6. Take a moment to send a message of gratitude to the water, and to the people who are working to ensure that clean water is available to all.

7. When you're ready, slowly open your eyes, and take a moment to reflect on the message of this meditation, and what steps you can take in your own life to support the access of clean water for all.

Note that access to clean water is a fundamental human right, and still many people around the world do not have access to it. Such meditations can help to raise awareness and inspire one to take actions to support organizations and individuals working to ensure that everyone has access to clean water.

WHO IS REALLY IN CHARGE?

Our bodies are made of 37.2 trillion cells.

We have 23 elements and 84 minerals in a constant
invisible exchange.

Even when we sleep, the waters of the world flow through us.

Each system, each part, each double-helix within is a rare
and miraculous life.

We eat the earth.

We poop the earth.

We are the earth.

Our teeth were once rocks.

Our toes were once seamoss.

Our mind's were once a beach.

Our hearts were once a mountainside.

With this proven scientific knowledge,

how can you be separate from me or anything?

Surrender in peace as you ask: who's really in charge?

NZAMBI MATEE

"We decided: what more can we do instead of just sitting on the sidelines and complaining."

Transforming crisis into opportunity is a fantabulous trait and should be recognized and rewarded everywhere possible. We all have that potential to live beyond fear and encourage such bravery. Take for example, Nzambi, who was a bright physicist, data expert and material engineer, who worked in the oil industry of Kenya before having a major change of heart.

In 2017, she quit her job as a data analyst in order to change the paradigm of waste and focus on sustainability. She set up a small laboratory in her mother's backyard. Creating and testing pavers, she tested for about a year in order to develop the right ratios for her paving bricks. She developed the first brick from plastic waste in 2018 and a year later in 2019, she made her own machine to convert plastic waste to bricks on a large scale. What a breakthrough for Kenya, the African continent and the world!

But she had quite a few challenges, such as the heavy labor involved, not to mention neighbors complaining about the noisy machinery. Given the long hours and need to focus single-pointedly, Matee stopped associating with her friends for a year; she was determined to carry out her mission no matter the sacrifice. Luckily, she won a scholarship to attend a social entrepreneurship training programme in the United States. During her tour to the USA, she used the material labs in the

University of Colorado Boulder to test and refine the ratios of sand to plastic.

She was heavily inspired to set up Gjenge Makers after witnessing the plastic bags being untidily scattered along the streets of Nairobi and choking local wildlife. Using her own design experience, she founded the startup company "Gjenge Makers" in order to recycle plastic waste into bricks. She designed her own machines at "Gjenge Maker" and her factory has recycled more than 20 tonnes of waste plastics as of 2021! The sturdy bricks - a mixture of plastic and sand - are both lighter and more durable than cement! Used to build walkways, her business now produces 1,500 pavers per day, while reducing the amount of plastic waste on the streets and in landfills. Because hindsight is 20/20, it's easy to appreciate Nzambi's innovations after her success, but it wasn't always so easy and we can't thank her enough for creating the solution needed to the crises she faced in her life and community. Here's to lifting up every Nzambi in every community around the globe!

A practical takeaway, inspired by Nzambi: how about organizing a grassroots environmental innovation challenge to address the issue of toxic materials across private or public sector industries? This challenge could be open to individuals, organizations, and companies, and could include a prize for the most promising or effective solutions. The challenge could also include mentorship and resources to support participants in further developing and implementing their ideas.

As a starting circle or facilitated introduction, here's a step-by-step guide to spark ideas or originality:

1. Gather a group of folks who are interested in solving the problem of toxic materials and repurposing them into useful, climate-friendly industrial products.

2. Begin the visualization by setting the intention to find innovative solutions for the problem at hand. Encourage the group to focus on positive and enthusiastic language and imagery. Encourage participants to close their eyes and take 10 deep breaths to relax and focus their minds.

3. Guide the group to visualize a world where the problem of toxic materials has been solved, and where these materials are being repurposed into useful, climate-friendly industrial products. Encourage participants to imagine the positive impact this would have on the environment, communities and the economy.

4. During these internal visualizations, allow participants to share their ideas and thoughts freely (NO BAD IDEAS!) on how to achieve this vision. Encourage the group to build off of each other's ideas and to think outside the box.

5. Encourage the group to continue nourishing and envisioning the potential solutions or the positive impact they would have on communities and the biosphere.

6. At the end of the visualization, encourage participants to open their eyes and to share their insights and ideas with the group. Encourage the group to continue discussing and developing their ideas until some feasible and implementable solutions are found.

7. Have a follow-up session (or multiple) to track the progress of the solutions and to continue brainstorming new ideas.

Again, it's paramount that this experience be done in a supportive and non-judgmental environment, where all ideas are welcome and encouraged.

THE WAY OF KINDNESS

The way of kindness
is built by moral collaboration,

needing constant reminders!

Collaboration is the ration,
the unity inside community;

Collaboration is how we
make kind babies (you and me);

Collaboration is how seeds dance wild for hours
with storms, creating wildflowers;

Collaboration is how art turns "eh" into "earth"
How plays on words create words on plays on words;

Collaboration is the time you thought you were stuck
on the roadside with a flat tire and no water - f*#@k!
But a stranger stopped to help and lift,
giving you everything you needed and a sandwich.

Why did the dolphin cross the road? To get to the other tide!
Why did the eagle cross the sky? To sip the wind and ride!

Collaboration is the click of dolphins and the nest of eagles.

Collaboration is built by caught dreams
the kindness we feel and show, when no one is watching.

How do you know the ocean is friendly? Because it waves!
How do you live the way of collaboration?
Because you are the way!

FATEMAH ALZELZELA

"I'm acting for nature…by exchanging waste for green space."

If at first they mock you, trust that you're probably doing something amazing and needed. That might have been an appropriate motto for Fatemah Alzelzela! Fatemah, the founder of Eco Star, a recycling and waste reduction company in Kuwait, who exemplifies the power of perseverance and determination in the face of skepticism and adversity. Despite facing initial skepticism from Kuwaiti authorities and potential business partners due to her age, gender and the social stigma surrounding waste collection in the country, Fatemah persisted and went on to win first place in a projects and innovation competition for her recycling and waste reduction idea.

Since launching in early 2019, her company Eco Star has made significant strides in tackling the waste crisis in Kuwait, recycling over 3.5 tons of plastic, 10 tons of paper, and 120 tons of metal. In a country where 90 percent of waste ends up in landfills, Fatemah's efforts have made a real impact on the environment. Additionally, she established an innovative partnership with a large nursery, where they give their customers shrubs and trees in exchange for their recycling from homes, restaurants, schools, and other businesses.

The statistics on waste in Kuwait are staggering: the country generates 1.5 kilograms of trash per person per day, twice the global average. Despite the provision of waste collection services

185

since the late 1960s, trash is handled by private companies with little screening or sorting, leading to pollution and disease. The lack of recycling is also a missed opportunity for the financial sector, as a 2014 study showed that 76 percent of Kuwait's waste is recyclable and the potential value of the raw materials that could be saved from dumps is over $130 million annually.

Fatemah's message is clear, "We are living on one planet, one environment, one land. Saving the environment means that you are going to save the future generation." Her unwavering commitment to her cause, despite the obstacles she faced, serves as an inspiration to others and a reminder that one person can make a real difference.

An innovative meditative practice inspired by the story of Fatemah Alzelzela and her company Eco Star could be called "The Eco-Star Benevolent Prank Meditation." This practice involves using visualization and mindfulness techniques to tap into one's own determination and creativity to come up with innovative solutions for recycling and reducing waste:

1. Begin by finding a quiet and comfortable space to sit in. Close your eyes and take a few deep breaths to relax and focus your mind.
2. Visualize yourself in the role of a recycling and waste reduction "Bioneer", just like Fatemah Alzelzela. Imagine yourself facing the same challenges and skepticism that she faced, but with the determination and perseverance to overcome them.
3. Imagine yourself walking through a landfill or a polluted area, and see the waste and pollution in your mind's eye. As you do this, start to manually pick up trash with gloves and fill a bag full of its contents. You can head

home to make something creative out of your findings - don't be grossed out even if it's hard!

4. Next, imagine you're making a call to a local political office or directly to one of the polluting companies or brands that were found as part of the trash in your clean-up. Why not go for it?! By all means necessary, find a way to set up a meeting with their leadership. Once you do, you can take whatever you made from the trash with you (ie. dress up as a giant trashed-human character?) and walk confidently into your local politician's offices (or company boardroom) with a videographer documenting and a lawyer representing by your side. Don't leave without delivering a demand to their leadership: a petition, a letter, a clear request to adjust practices, policies or laws so that their supply chain is improved with real accountability. They'll make more money by doing so anyway!

5. Allow your mind to wander and come up with creative ideas and solutions for this recycling and reducing waste prank. Let your imagination run wild in the positive impact that these implemented demands or solutions would have on the environment and your community.

6. As you continue to visualize, focus on the feeling of determination and the willingness to take action to make a difference. Now, when you feel ready, open your eyes and take a few extra deep breaths. Write down any insights that came to you during the meditation, and consider how you can turn them into action.

This fun practice can help to tap into the determination and creativity needed to come up with innovative solutions for recycling and reducing waste. It could also help to cultivate a sense of compassion and a desire to make a difference in the world, similar to Fatemah Alzelzela's. It's important to remember that this is a personal practice, so you should customize it to your own needs and adapt it to your own situation.

I vs WE

I is for illness

We is for wellness

I is illusion of separation

We is for wowing all nations

I once thought lying wasn't ignorant

Had to ask the we for forgiveness

Got put in my place and told me I'm not alone

I'm a link in the infinite chain of existence

And just cause my eye's in the sun

Doesn't mean my shadow won't distract the lightness

Are my eyes watching God or the distraction?

Are we gods or just an ego seeking attention?

Maybe it's both but only with humble integration

Time to live in this world but not of it!

The I in the we is the best life hack trick

It's the all in one, one in all collection

It's how we come together, hearts wide open

I for inspiration, now merging with the infinite ocean

The wave remembers its origin

The self becomes God pouring in.

PAUL STAMETS

"MycoDiversity is BioSecurity."

Once upon a toadstool, a world of human imagination was born! As we first consumed these fungal realms, did we learn to think in symbiotic partnership with our earth and mushroom friends? Did humanity's evolution get spurred by the consuming of fungi (especially the psychedelic) and did they play a crucial role in the development of the human mind and culture? When you consider that "we are what we eat", it's not such a radical notion since so many ancient (and more recent) villages were built around the practicality and sanctity of mushrooms · psychedelic or not. They have nutritional and ecological benefits that go far and beyond what we might now even imagine, let alone know definitively. And one of the biggest champions of this vast toadstool world is the great Mr. Paul Stamets.

A mycologist, medical researcher and entrepreneur, Paul is considered an intellectual and industry leader in fungi: habitat, medicinal use, and production. Since being inspired by his older brother to explore this wild world, he has voraciously studied the organisms that literally exist under every footstep taken on this path of life. He now researches, protects, propagates and publishes cutting edge work demonstrating how mushroom species can help heal the health of people & planet. One of the core thesis' is that ecosystems have "immune systems, just like people, and mushrooms are the cellular bridges between the two".

"We are now fully engaged in the sixth Major Extinction ("6 X")
on planet Earth. Our biosphere is quickly changing, eroding the
life support systems that have allowed humans to ascend.
Unless we put into action policies and technologies that can
cause a course correction in the very near future, species
diversity will continue to plummet, with humans not only being
the primary cause, but one of the victims. What can we do?
Fungi, particularly mushrooms, offer some powerful, practical
solutions, which can be put into practice now.

Here are a few mycoremediation (a form of bioremediation in
which fungi-based methods are used to decontaminate the
environment) challenges that our dear reader can employ
immediately:

1. Start a mushroom cultivation project in your backyard or
    local community garden. Research different types of
    mushrooms that have the ability to break down
    pollutants and toxins, such as oyster mushrooms,
    shiitake, or reishi. Grow these mushrooms in a controlled
    environment and monitor their ability to break down
    pollutants in the soil.
2. Conduct a mycoremediation project in your local park or
    nature reserve. Work with a team of volunteers to
    identify areas of the park that are contaminated with
    pollutants such as oil, pesticides, or heavy metals.
    Research which types of mushrooms are best suited for
    breaking down these pollutants and implement a
    mushroom cultivation program in the affected area.
3. Conduct a home-based mycoremediation project by
    creating a mushroom compost in your own backyard.
    Research how to create a compost that is rich in nutrients
    and can support the growth of mushrooms. Once the
    compost is ready, inoculate it with mushroom spores and

monitor the growth of the mushrooms. When the mushrooms have grown, use them to break down pollutants in your own backyard.

4. Research and test the effectiveness of using mushrooms to break down pollutants in water. Look into different types of mushrooms that can be grown in water-based environments and test their ability to break down pollutants such as oil, pesticides, or heavy metals in a controlled environment.

5. Start a mushroom cultivation project in your school or community center. Use this as an opportunity to educate people about the power of mushrooms in breaking down pollutants and the importance of mycoremediation in protecting our environment.

These are just a few examples of the many potential mycoremediation experiments that can be put into practice now for the good of your local ecosystem. The key is to be creative and come up with your own ideas for projects that will make a positive impact on the environment in your community.

BACK TO THE GARDEN

So wild was earth's old
wonderworld-underworld, so fresh & soaked
Once we thought we saw two microbes eloped!
We laughed as goofy bantered teenagers -
Like... if we want more youth in organic agriculture
Let's talk about all the sex below our toes!
Why is soil dirtier than porn but less popular?
Because desire is manipulated like jokes
And we aren't attracted to bugs or tropes?
But with every seed and sensual touch,
the fertility of the earth becomes a body of quotes:
Femme furrows as his highness sows the royal oats!
Nitrogen & carbon roots & grows in loads.
Profane becomes sacred in these naked portraits - whoa! -
like Basquiat, O'Keefe or Picasso.
Or Hafiz & Angelou in every terra firma scroll.
Mycelial networks - Web 0.0
- NFTree troves - dialed-in before AOL!
Our hands, hearts and loins taught us to love this earth home.

When nature was our nurture, design and mold
Back to the future, NOW is the best time to plant & grow
Build organic matter, make that money, bread & dough
Economical comes from ecological
Green like plants, ROI better than a JP Morgan portfolio
As humans from the humus, we can stop to go
Back to the garden ... or else we will lose it all.

REBEL QUESTIONS

Life will always have challenges, but challenges can't compete with the evolutionary gift of existence. Yes, the forms we exist within are impermanent. Yes, that's hard. But change is a blessing, if we are kind and courageous with ourselves through the process. Life lives on ecstatically, even through our challenges or changes, going beyond our finite existence in these spacesuit bodies of ours. At our core, we are energy and energy constantly transforms. We transfer our energy into new forms, in new times and spaces, like a starling bird murmuration changing shapes through the sunset. And there are infinite forms life can take. It can be scary but fear is just false evidence appearing real. In such moments, remember not to tell God (or Dog, depending who you worship) about how big your fears are, but tell your fears about how big your God (Dog) is!

Some questions for all of us as we expand our proverbial wings into a kinder planetary jet stream:

Have we ever dared to imagine a life we truly want to have? One that uplifts (and levitates) for ourselves, others and the planet? What about a life that is unreasonably beautiful and awesome?

How do we fortify ourselves and our communities in realizing an ecozoic era on earth? What if we used our vast resources, engineering, craftsmanship and intelligence for such a noble, profitable and respectful mission?

How can we encourage and proliferate a culture of kindness within our businesses, governments, schools and family units? Can we create a global movement for, of and by loving-kindness ... starting with ourselves, in the intimacy of our everyday lives?

We need kindness to go viral - or spiral - spreading like a tonic contagion ever, faster than any virus. It starts with you and me, becoming the almighty we. Kindness makes life the best possible for the most possible. People and the planet can thrive in ways we once thought we could only dream of. And that's the beauty of being humans: we can manifest our inner thoughts into a shared reality! Let's manifest the positive dreams and put the negative ones that don't serve us to rest.

Our actions, large or small, all add up to make an impact. Like a sacred and interlocking geometric design, all things are connected and all touchpoints matter. And through conscious perspectives and wise choices, we can reconnect these dots to empower ourselves, our families and the natural world.

If we are to mend our present selves and realize that a willingness to kill over resources will only hinder our chances for repairing the biosphere, then let the change start yesterday. If we believe in preserving life, we must use our heart-minds and become good ancestors to every living thing. Ultimately, no matter what our background is, we can ask ourselves: "if not us then who, and if not now, then when?"

In many wisdom traditions, it is said to "look first to the kingdom within and all shall be given" or "the highest God and the innermost God is one God." Sages also remind us of the importance of a beginner's mind to stay open and receptive to life's changing nature. This inner focus shifts our paradigm from obsessing over feeble attempts to control external conditions and allows us to take our power back. This isn't an aggressive, violent or hierarchical power but rather a power that yields peace, success, kindness and health in the body, mind and spirit. This kingdom or God or sense of inner peace (the descriptor isn't important) is inside each of us, awaiting exploration and realization. All it takes is a willingness to care for the infinite being that we call life.

SLOWPOKE

In a forgotten animal kingdom, a wise old tortoise named Slowpoke saw a young rabbit named Thumper rushing through the forest, always in a hurry and stepping on baby plants or insects with no regard for the sanctity of life. Slowpoke noticed that Thumper never seemed to stop racing around and was as stressed as a pet rabbit in an invisible cage.

One day, Slowpoke saw Thumper struggling angrily to carry a heavy load of carrots back to his burrow. Slowpoke offered to help, and Thumper reluctantly agreed. Together, they walked back to Thumper's place. Along the way, Slowpoke gasped joyfully at the beauty of the forest: "What if we could hear the music of springtime flowers and see the paintings of birdsong? What if we could taste the dancing of the mushroom and tree roots under our toes? Isn't life always interdepen-dancing all around?" Strangely, Thumper felt his heartbeat slow down for the first time since his mother died from a terrible hunting incident! He began to awkwardly appreciate the small things that he had been too busy to notice before: a family of ferns doing mathematics in the breeze, a beaver restoring a riverway and an aspen tree growing a garden with friends.

When they arrived at Thumper's burrow, Slowpoke helped him unload the carrots and made sure he was comfortable before saying goodbye. Thumper thanked Slowpoke for his help and realized that he had been missing out on the simple pleasures of life. From that day on, Thumper made a conscious effort to slow down and enjoy the beauty of the forest. He visited Slowpoke often, and they would sit and talk about life, enjoying each other's company. "Why is it always the tortoise vs the hare? Why not just the tortoise hanging out with the hare!" joked Slowpoke in a gregarious belly laugh.

One day, Thumper fell ill, and he was unable to leave his burrow. Slowpoke knew how much Thumper relied on him, so he took it upon himself to care for his young friend. He visited Thumper every day, brought him medicine and food, and kept him company.

Thanks to Slowpoke's kindness and care, Thumper made a full recovery. Thumper was grateful for Slowpoke's help and realized that he needed to truly slow down and learn the art of loving-care or he'd miss the whole point. Doh!

Witnessing this slow transformation of Thumper, many other creatures in the forest were inspired by Slowpoke's kindness, and his story became a legend in the forgotten animal kingdom. Animal schoolchildren were even taught in school, "Be like Slowpoke, always ready to lend a helping paw to those in need, and to remind us to slow down and enjoy the beauty of life. Life honors those who honor life."

~ AUTHOR STATEMENTS ~

AARON'S STORY

Growing up in a "My way or the Highway" society, I often felt like a fish trying to climb a tree. My slippery relationship with conformity was beyond difficult, especially since I was a feminine boy, athlete poet and raised on an organic farm in the middle of a city. I remember being forced to eat my natural homemade lunches in the bathroom to dodge the fast-food-sponsored school bullies. Though I shined as a star on the sports fields, I awkwardly snuck away in secret to write love poems or romantic comedy skits during halftimes. While my friends kept stats on the latest celebrity scandals, I kept stats on my breath, learning the science of yoga to calm my teenage angst and concern for the fall of civilization. I felt like a "figure eight" of contradictions circling around for acceptance from a world built for boxes and cookie cutters. Fortunately, before turning to drugs or gangs, I had some maladjusted family and overly-kind mentors interrupt my growing obsession with being liked to give me a simple message: **you can embrace your unique self as a gift and a blessing, just as you are!**

Because of this multi-hyphenate reality, I found myself bridgebuilding and navigating life between the margins and across community lines. I played peacemaker between rival gangs on the soccer field or at the local hip-hop cipher, learning that playing and praying was more fun than getting played and preyed on. At farmers markets, I counseled celebrities and the homeless (often together) on healthy eating habits or how to heal the soil-food web - simply by organic gardening. By the time I was 18, I had already traveled extensively, serving many environmental programs and supporting humanitarian organizations with a joyful heart.

Through these experiences, I learned the importance of kindness as a foolproof tool to get out of trouble! Because humility, listening and creativity were my best escape tactics from tough situations, I latched onto goodwill as a lifeboat and compass. Even better, I started to realize a similar type of loving-kindness emanating from family, friends and community members. If only I could tell you how many times I was bailed out from a hairy scenario or given a gift that saved my butt! This cycle of genuine compassion, often without repayment, has given me an unconditional faith in life's inherent benevolence.

Now, many decades later, I have endless stories of rebellious big-heartedness, all of which has shown me that the world has more caring people than mean jerks. I now raise my young daughter to encourage her to "look for the helpers", "find the kind" or "aspire to inspire before you expire!" It all starts at home with daily practices that ripple out into projects like *Rebels Of Kindness*.

In a time when divisiveness, war, and planetary emergencies run rampant, everyday principles like kindness reconnect us to our purpose and a protopian vision for our world. The so-called weirdos, the rebels and the outcasts (like those scribbled throughout the pages of this book) are helping us see our way back to what truly matters. We can reclaim our sovereign birthright as "human kind", coexisting on this rare paradise floating through the universe.

JUSTIN'S STORY

My parents, Holly and Jason Wilkenfeld, were the trailblazers of kindness in my life. They went against the norm in the 70s, as white people adopting children of color in a society still recovering from a challenging time in civil rights history. My parents were so different, coming from Jewish and Christian families, one an artist from upstate New York, and the other a future PhD physicist. They were an unlikely mix for a family, but it was clear that their love and kindness towards each other and their children was the foundation of our family.

After meeting my beloved wife and having our kids, we went through the typical caterpillar to butterfly experience of our identity changing from "I" to "We". We went from accumulation and worldly success to giving and operating from love. This has been the core tenet and compass for our lives and work.

When we founded Kindhumans, a public benefit corporation, and the associated Kindhumans Media Foundation, Inc, and Rebels of Kindness projects, our goal was to amplify the voices and efforts of individuals working to make the world a better place. These people may have had to challenge the status quo, go against the norm, or use their skills, platforms, and experiences to help society improve. Our aim is to shine a light on those working to improve lives and fill gaps for those in need.

In this kind-hearted creation with Aaron, we are also asking deeper questions about the human potential:

Why do we continue to engage in so much conflict in this interconnected and globalized world, when there are so many more important and fascinating things that we could be focusing on? We are often consumed by our own biases and dogma, preventing us from continuing to grow and evolve as humans in a connected society. We become entrenched in our perspectives, and we feel insecure when someone disagrees or does things differently. We engage in endless debates, trying to prove others wrong or ourselves right. Even when we know we are wrong, we often try to save face or hold on to our position stubbornly. This is simply human nature. People are imperfect and yet, most of us try our best to live a good life. We all want to have enough to shift from just surviving to thriving, and from there we can strive to make the world a better place.

And what is a better place if it's not made from love? Love is the ultimate guide, and kindness is the greatest action we can take as we navigate this complex and beautiful life. Finding the path to kindness towards others, our planet, and ourselves is something that I hope all of the nearly 8 billion people on earth strive for. It's a collective effort, one that requires effort from both the bottom and the top. We need to empower all people to act with kindness.

However, it can be difficult to find role models for kindness in today's world. The media often focuses on showing the worst aspects of humanity and neglects to highlight the positive change-makers working towards the greater good. This constant bombardment of negative news is overwhelming and needs to change. We need to shift our attention towards those who embody one of our greatest characteristics as humans - kindness. Kindness is action, it takes effort and it is thoughtful, generous, and comes from a place of compassion within every human being on the planet.

CONTACT

For more information on Kindhumans Foundation,
please visit www.kindhumansfoundation.org
or email info@kindhumansfoundation.org

For more info on Kindhumans,
the for-profit marketplace of eco-friendly products,
please visit www.kindhumans.com

For more info on Aaron Ableman,
please visit www.aaronableman.com
or email aaroneableman@gmail.com

Printed in the USA
CPSIA information can be obtained
at www.ICGtesting.com
JSHW080720221123
52377JS00001B/1